A LITTLE COOKING, A LITTLE TALKING AND A WHOLE LOT OF FUN

WITH FLORENCE HENDERSON

AND FRIENDS FROM HER KRAZY COUNTRY KITCHEN

Written by Florence Henderson
Edited by Elyssa A. Harte

1st Edition 1988

PANORAMA PUBLISHING COMPANY

14640 Victory Boulevard, Suite 210
Van Nuys, CA 91411

First Edition
Copyright © 1988 by JFK Marketing, Inc.

Library of Congress Cataloging-in-Publication Data

Henderson, Florence,
    A little cooking, a little talking, and a whole lot of fun.

    Includes index.
    1. Cookery.   2. Country kitchen (Television program)
I. Harte, Elyssa A., 1952-   . II. Title.
TX715.H495   1988   641.5   87-32711
ISBN 0-937671-74-6 (pbk.)

Published by
PANORAMA PUBLISHING COMPANY
14640 Victory Boulevard
Van Nuys, CA 91411
(818) 988-4690

Cover Design by Blumhoff Design
Design and Typography by Premiere Concepts
Printing by Delta Lithograph

DEDICATION

To my husband, John, who has given
me the recipe for happiness.

ACKNOWLEDGEMENTS

To my producers, Allen Reid and Mady Land, without whom, of course, there could not have been a show, much less a book; your unending support and direction has been wonderful. To all my guests, thank you for making each show so special and so much fun; I truly enjoyed working with each one of you.

To all the Reid/Land Productions' staff, thanks again; your help has been invaluable. My thanks also to the crew of Country Kitchen, Ginger Walsh and her staff, and to my staff, Chris Vick, Sarah Rosenberg, Roger Fogleman and Ted Schwarz.

And special thanks to my editor, Elyssa Harte.

Table of Contents

Foreword . . . . *ix*

The Making of
"Country Kitchen" 1

The Guests:

Willie Nelson 9

   Country Gravy 11

Jim Varney 13

   Curry Pepper Steak 15

Irlene Mandrell 17

   Steak Stew 19

The Bellamy Brothers 21

   Stir-Fry Shrimp 23

Ricky Skaggs 25

   Country Breakfast 27

Dottie West 29

   Stuffed Bell Peppers 31

George Lindsey 33

   Barbecued Chicken
   and Cole Slaw 35

B.J. Thomas 37

   Fettucini Alfredo 39

Darrell Waltrip 41

   Fish Florentine 43

Tanya Tucker 45

   Dorito Chip Salad 47

Ralph Emery 49

   Cheeseburger Noodles 51

Don Gay 55

   Texas Tacos 57

Barry Williams 59

   Stuffed Cornish Game Hens . . . 61

Larry Gatlin 63

   Tortilla Soup 65

Jim Nabors 67

   Chinese Chicken Salad 69

Jeannie C. Riley 73

   Texas Hot Tamale Pie 75

Richard Sterban 77

   Lasagna 79

Minnie Pearl 81

   Creole Egg Casserole 83

Robert Reed 85

   Beef and Biscuit Casserole 87

Mel Tillis 89

   Country Summer
   Day Dinner 91

Harry Blackstone, Jr. 93

   Steak 95

Shelly West 97

   Wiener Schnitzel 99

The Whites 101

   Chicken Enchiladas 103

Joe Bonsall 105

   Italian
   Eggplant Casserole 107

Della Reese 109

   Broccoli Chicken Thighs 111

T. Graham Brown 113

   Cheesy "Spam" Bake 115

Freddie Fender 117

   Migas Rancheras 119

David Frizzell 123

   Enchiladas Verdes 125

Eddie Rabbitt 127

   Beef Bombay 129

Barbara Eden 131

   Lamb Ka-Bob 133

Jerry Clower 135

   Mississippi Fried Chicken 137

Orville Redenbacher 141

   Italian Chicken 143

Jim Ed Brown 145

   Wild Duck Casserole 147

Jimmy Dean 149

   Fall-Baked Apples 151

Michael Johnson 153

   Chili Beef Stir-Fry 155

Johnny Tillotson 157

  Salmon with
   Lemon Basil Sauce 159

T.G. Sheppard 161

  Chicken and Shrimp
   Supreme 163

Sharon White 165

   Pork 'n' Kraut 167

Dan Seals 169

   Homestyle Potato Soup 171

Sylvia 173

   Spaghetti 175

Hoyt Axton 177

  Hamburger a la Brandy
   and Potato Chips 179

John McEuen 181

   Nitty Gritty Dirt Chicken 183

Bobby Bare 185

   Wild Rice and Shrimp 187

Phyllis Diller 189

   Fish Fillets Dijon 191

Johnny Lee 193

   Mustard Bass 195

Jeff Cook 197

  Japanese Shrimp
   and Vegetables 199

Bill Anderson 201

   Whispering Jambalaya 203

John Sebastian 205

   Spaghetti alla Carbonara 207

Johnny Rodriguez 209

   Carne Guisada 211

Rosey Grier 213

   File Gumbo 215

Faron Young 217

   Hillbilly Stew 219

Jimmy Walker 221

   Barbecued Spareribs 223

Index 225

Foreword

Before I met Florence Henderson, I knew of her only as a talented and sophisticated lady of Broadway. Then I met her and found two new words to describe her — country... and mischievous.

Finding out that Florence was born and raised a country girl was a surprise to me. Besides a love of entertaining, we now had something else in common. Thus, learning of her country background endeared her even more to me.

And mischievous? Well, over the several years we've been friends, she's surprised me more than once with her candor and wit. I remember once, after a show, we went to a restaurant to relax, have coffee and talk. We wanted to get away from all the music ringing in our ears. Little did we know when we picked the place that we'd have strolling violins literally surrounding us. But knowing how important respect and appreciation is to all entertainers, we said nothing... at first. But they kept on and on... and on, lavishing us with song after song and no break in sight.

When at last they stopped long enough to ask us if we would like them to do anything special for us, my mouth fell open as I heard Florence gently say, "Yes, we'd like you to 'take five'," a show business term for *take a break*! She was so gentle, though, they understood and went away, happy to have played for us.

In addition to being outspoken, Florence loves the element of surprise. She had me reeling in laughter once after my performance of the song, "Gypsy Rose." At the end of the song, I usually bring people from the audience up on stage, give them each a long boa and get them to "bump and grind" to the music. We all laugh and have a good time and that's how it ends.

This time, I turned to give the conductor my signal to end the number, and all of a sudden the audience went wild with laughter, and the conductor kept right on playing. I turned to see what had happened, thinking maybe someone had lost a piece of clothing or something, and I see Florence standing there in her bathrobe, grinning at me.

Before I could even react, she began slipping her bathrobe down off her shoulders while dancing across the stage. Now, while this was clearly a humorous strip tease, I was rendered speechless. Florence had had wardrobe make her a "costume" for this number — short shorts and a skimpy top.

She danced over to me, playfully rubbed my leg and my mouth dropped open even wider. With my every reaction, the audience laughed even more. Then she simply danced away, swinging her bathrobe in time with the music, and left the stage without saying a single word! By the time I recovered and found my voice again, she was gone.

Another side of Florence, her serious side, practices many wise philosophies of life. Perhaps it is because she has known pain and unhappiness for part of her younger life that she has taken the time to learn and apply the lessons of how to get and keep success and happiness so well.

So, Florence is a fun person, spontaneous and frank, understanding and compassionate — all qualities that make her a good interviewer. Florence makes you feel comfortable and at ease, able to open up and talk freely.

This book conveys those same traits. It's fun, open and honest, spontaneous and upbeat. Its serious side is generous, compassionate and wise.

Florence has said that God gave her two talents — one to give the gift of entertainment and one to be a mother. I'd like to add, Florence, you have one more talent — to give the gift of friendship so well.

Enjoy Florence and her friends in *A Little Cooking, A Little Talking and A Whole Lot of Fun.* She's a remarkable lady. It's a remarkable book.

Jim Nabors
November, 1987

WELCOME TO MY COUNTRY KITCHEN!

The Making of Country Kitchen

Country Kitchen, my television show on The Nashville Network, is a dream come true for me. I have long wanted a talk show and was thrilled when my manager called to tell me that there was an opportunity in Nashville. Wesson Oil, the chief sponsor of the program, had also requested my involvement.

My excitement was high when I began working in Nashville. First, there was the thrill not only of having the show but of knowing that Wesson Oil was involved. The company has been extremely good to me and I have been doing commercials for them for more than ten years. That may not mean much to most of you, but when someone is asked to be the spokesperson for a product, as I have been for Wesson Oil, their involvement is usually quite short. Advertising agencies change, management changes, and everyone usually wants to make his or her mark on the way a product is sold. An individual who works as spokesperson one week may discover that he or she is no longer wanted the next week. To be with a product as long as I have been with Wesson Oil means that you are doing something right and that your efforts are respected. It is a wonderful feeling and a wonderful trust.

The other pleasure I encountered at the start came from learning about the people of Nashville. I have worked in New York and Hollywood for most of what I've done on television. I have been on Broadway and worked in the major nightclubs around the country. But I had never known Nashville as a major center for television production and had no idea what the crew would be like. Since the quality of the crew determines the real success of a show, I was rather nervous about what I might be facing.

I shouldn't have worried. The producer, director, technical crew, make-up people, and everyone else were all wonderful. They are top professionals, highly skilled, and equal to the best anywhere in the country.

For those of you who have watched my program from the start, you have undoubtedly recognized the evolution of the program. When we first started, we used to "wing it" quite a bit. For example, there was a woman named Bev Porter who played the piano for me. We would rehearse the music only briefly, which did not give me all the preparation I realized I wanted. Sometimes the music was flawless, other times I felt it could have been better. I feel that no matter what an entertainer is doing, no matter whether the person is volunteering or being paid, he or she should always give 100%. Without more careful planning, I felt there were times when I was not reaching that goal.

Bev was unable to spend more time because of other commitments so, reluctantly, we arranged for Tim Hubler to take over. Tim is a brilliant young musician and ours has been a good association.

What I do now is go to Nashville three or four days before we tape. First I meet with the producer and other people involved with the preparation of the show. Then I meet with Tim Hubler so we can go over all the music. We set keys, trying to decide what keys will work best for the guests. In the meantime, the producers will have talked with the guests about the songs they would like to do. Thus, we work on the specific music we will be using.

There are other concerns as well. How does my hair look? If there is a problem, Cheryl Riddle, my hairdresser, will give me a perm.

What do I know about the guests? We arrange to obtain as much background material as we can get, even when the guest is a long time friend. I try to learn as much as I can so I'm able to prepare questions that I think will be interesting to both myself and the audience. This also lets me be spontaneous because I will have an awareness of whatever aspect of the person's life the guest wants to discuss.

When we begin production, we usually do three shows a day. This allows me and my guest to make the most effective use of our time. However, to work this way also requires a lot of thought, planning, concentration and energy from everyone involved. It also requires a top professional crew because, otherwise, such a volume of work could not be completed.

I get up very early on the day of taping, wash my hair, grab a cup of coffee, and eat a light breakfast because there is no time for anything more. As I dress, I consider my questions and go over the way in which I will do the show. Then I go from the Sheraton Music City Hotel to Opry Land where The Nashville Network Studios are located. Once there, I have another cup of coffee while Cheryl does my hair.

Cheryl is one of those extremely dedicated, delightful individuals. She is always willing to come in on her day off, work late, and do whatever is necessary to make certain everything is done right. I call her a magician because she can put your hair in dozens of different ways and always make it look good. Even on those days when I come in and my hair seems out of control, in a few minutes she has it styled perfectly, something I would have thought impossible.

When Cheryl is finished, Joyce Daniel comes in. Joyce is

Hairdresser Cheryl Riddle working her "magic."

the best make-up artist in Nashville and equal to the best I've seen anywhere.

Some make-up artists are almost eccentric about their craft. They look upon your face as a blank canvas which they must have all to themselves. If you do anything yourself, even so much as adding your own base in order to save time, they become extremely upset. Joyce, on the other hand, figures that if the person with whom she is working wants to do some of the make-up herself, there is

Joyce Daniel doing makeup for Florence's guest, Randy Travis.

a chance that they know something more about themselves than she does. Instead of being jealous or angry, Joyce assumes that she may learn something new and is delighted with the opportunity.

Joyce is also sensitive to my moods and the moods of others who may need make-up. There are times you want to talk, times you wish to be silent. Joyce understands this and respects it.

Ken Vincent, our director, is an extremely competent, quiet, mild-mannered man. He is the person who sits in the control booth, guiding the camera operators. He determines the angles, the speed with which the cameras will respond to changes in the show, and generally creates what you see on the screen. Unlike many directors, he doesn't yell and scream at the people on the set to get what he wants done.

Likewise, Allen Reid, our producer, is an extremely competent individual and has been a great help in booking harder-to-reach guests, such as Willie Nelson.

Terry Ree and Bruce Williams are the guys who give all the dessert recipes on the show. They will rehearse each recipe to make certain they are familiar with what they will be doing. Terry is a Sioux Indian and a tenor who hails from Pierre, South Dakota. Bruce Williams, who calls himself "the white guy," is from Mountain Home, Idaho, and plays bass. Together they are called Williams and Ree.

They met at Black Hills State college, which they describe as "a perennial national collegiate powerhouse in nothing!" So they claim that, "After majoring in such diverse curriculum as registration and draft-dodging, we decided to pursue a career in comedy."

Today Williams and Ree are opening acts for such major entertainers as The Oak Ridge Boys, Mel Tillis, Roy Clark, and others. They appear throughout the United States and have several albums including a recent one entitled, "Feed and Mingle With Live Indians." They also write most of their own material. Bruce Williams and Terry Ree are two very talented guys.

Tim Hubler on piano, Florence, Randy Travis and David Owens on camera.

David Owens, one of the cameramen for the show has been with us since the beginning and is excellent at his work. We actually use a total of four cameras plus other special equipment.

Depending upon the time we have, there may be a brief rehearsal of the songs to be sung. How much rehearsing we can do at this stage will vary with the day and how tight our schedule might be.

While we rehearse, Tim Hubler is on piano, but playing piano is not Tim's only talent — he plays a variety of musical instruments well and is incredibly talented and versatile.

When the song is unfamiliar to either myself or the guest, we will use cue cards. Zelda and Margaret both hold cards for me and work with the show, "Nashville Now," as well. They are incredibly efficient, working fast and keeping up with the camera positions so we are always able to see them.

Zelda on cue cards.

Billy Paul Jones, Associate Producer; Billy Turner, Stage Manager; Florence and Randy Travis.

Another talent, Billy Turner, our stage manager, is the man I consider to be the mainstay of our staff. He coordinates everything between the control booth and the floor. He wears a headset and quietly talks with everyone involved. He gives me all my signals, telling me how much time I have to talk, whether I should speed up or slow down. I constantly rely upon him for help. Billy is also the one who comes to get me when we're ready for rehearsal and production.

After Williams and Ree have rehearsed their dessert segment, Billy will alert me to the fact that we are ready for music. Then I meet with him, Billy Paul Jones, the associate producer, Tim Hubler, and our guest for the day. Billy Paul Jones makes many of the arrangements for booking our guests and is a singer in his own right (and is quite popular with the ladies). During this pre-production stage, we all work to make certain the music we have chosen and the key we have selected will be appropriate for the guest.

Ken Vincent, Director; Terry Ree and Bruce Williams of Williams and Ree; and Allen Reid, Producer.

After rehearsing the song, I return to my dressing room, dress and handle last minute touches for my hair and make-up. At that time, the guest rehearses the cooking segment with Billy Paul Jones and Ginger Walsh, our food stylist. I purposely do not involve myself in the cooking rehearsal because I want to be able to act spontaneously. If I know what is going to happen, everything begins to look pat and that can be boring. As Dean Martin once said about television, you don't want to rehearse *too* much because you'll

Assorted staff, cameras and crew during rehearsal.

Ginger Walsh, our food stylist; Randy Travis and Billy Paul Jones.

get too good and nobody will want to watch you. I don't know if I agree completely, but I do feel there's some truth to it.

Ginger Walsh is the person we all talk about on the show. She has beautiful red hair and green eyes and is a dynamite lady. She is a gentle person who works extremely hard, yet with a wonderful attitude. She gives our guests great confidence because they are not expert cooks. She is vitally important to the show.

Florence and Sarah Rosenberg, her assistant.

As I dress, last minute preparations take place. The entire crew prepares equipment and takes their positions, the overhead mirror is prepared for special photographs, and last minute instructions are given.

Meanwhile, Sarah Rosenberg, my assistant, helps me pick out my clothing and helps with the dressing. Because we will work on 13 shows at a time, I need 13 different outfits. I wear a size 2, which is not easy to find, and Sarah will often have shopped for the outfits I wear.

Next, Billy Turner will come to tell me we are ready to begin. At this point, I am always nervous, and I remind myself it's only the anticipation of the unknown that I feel. Because there's a live audience and I want everything to be the best, I'm thinking, "will it all come together, or will it not?" It usually does, and as soon as we start rolling, I'm fine.

After a last touch-up to make-up from Joyce, Billy will introduce us, and my guest and I will usually walk out together. I will say a few words, then we will sit down at the table and wait for the opening music and taping to begin.

You may have noticed what seem to be still photographs shown on the screen at the beginning of each show. There will be one of me, one of my guest, and one of Williams and Ree. What you may not know is that these are not still photographs. These are live images for which we have to sit perfectly still, as though they are individual photographs.

Then there is the count-down and the show begins.

For each show, there is iced tea in front of myself and my guest, a drink most of us prefer. What my guests do not always realize is that the tea is real but the ice is a plastic prop. Real ice cubes melt too fast for the hot lights. The plastic cubes are for decoration and the liquid is warm!

During the show, Ken Vincent and his assistant are in the control room. Here they watch the show on a main monitor, and on individual monitors for each camera. They watch the smaller screens to position the cameras for each shot then cut to those cameras. They not only watch what you see at home, they watch the ways they can move to different camera positions. These changes in camera viewpoint add variety to what you see and thus, increase your enjoyment of the program.

The program overall is a delight. We try to tape each show without a break or a retaping. We'll do one show, have lunch, do a second show, take a break, and tape the third. It is exhausting work but great fun and the food we have made during the show disappears very quickly. As well, we have a caterer who prepares additional food for the cast and crew.

At the end of the day, after taping three shows, we return to the Sheraton Music City where invariably friends or family come by to visit. Often we will have a drink in the lobby bar, a beautiful place where Linda Scott, the wife of one of our production staff, entertains. I always enjoy listening to new singers and here, I relax while enjoying her performance.

This same schedule will continue each day until the 13 shows have been completed. Although it's a tiring schedule, it is all so enjoyable, I hope that Country Kitchen is around for many years to come.

Control room with Director, Ken Vincent, and his assistant.

Willie Nelson

I was delighted to have Willie Nelson as a guest for my show. Everyone had told me that he was too busy or that he didn't do things like that, but I knew I wanted him to appear. Thus, I kept prodding my producer and even went to the president of the Nashville Network who knows Willie well.

Eventually, much to my delight, Willie agreed to appear. Then I was told that he would not be cooperative and certainly would not sing a song. Yet, Willie was a quiet gentleman. He said he would sing as many songs as I wanted. He arrived early so he would cause no problems, even though the night before he was the host for "Saturday Night Live," an engagement that meant flying half the night. He is a true professional.

Willie is an unusual man, extremely quiet and shy, yet very much a nonconformist. He walked into the studio wearing a sweat shirt and blue jeans, his hair in a pigtail, an earring in one ear. Yet no matter how he looks, he has an inner magnetism that has a tremendous appeal for women.

Willie's introduction to music was rather unusual. He was raised by his grandparents who, as they learned about music themselves, taught both Willie and his sister, Bobbie Lee. However, it seems that instead of taking lessons from a musician, Willie's grandparents learned music from mail order courses.

My own father believed in items sold through mail order as well. His favorite purchases were usually patent medicines. In fact, when I was 14 and had an appendicitis attack, he tried to treat it by giving me all the various patent medicines he had obtained through the mail. He assumed it was just a stomach ache, though fortunately I got to a hospital before the damage was so serious that my life was threatened.

Of course, when I grew up, mail order catalogs served multiple purposes. My family always had an outhouse, a sophisticated "two holer," so the Sears, Roebuck Catalog provided an important, inexpensive source of toilet paper!

Another similarity between Willie and myself is that my parents loved music as did his grandparents. I still remember awakening in the morning and hearing my father singing a spiritual. And my mother learned to play piano, guitar, and the jew's harp by ear.

I was always proud of my mother's ability, but rather naive about the instruments. I talked in school about my mother playing the harp, not realizing that there was a difference between the big stringed instrument and the jew's harp. The latter is a small instrument about 3 inches in length. The lyre-shaped frame is held in the teeth while a metal tongue is plucked to make music.

The priest heard me talking and wondered if my mother would come and play her "harp" in church. I said I thought she would and, when I asked her, she never realized that I had not explained the exact nature of her instrument. As a result, she showed up as requested, carrying her small jew's harp, surprising everyone.

For those of us who grew up poor and in the country, music was an important part of our lives. At least it was for those of us who were lucky.

Willie had a variety of odd jobs when he first started out. He worked in 1956 as a disc jockey, using that position to sell a self-financed record, "No Place For Me," to his listeners in Vancouver, Washington. He also became a door-to-door salesman of encyclopedias, Bibles, and other items. Sadly, when he began to do club work in Houston, Texas, he was so poor that he sold some of his early work for almost nothing. His song "Family Bible" went for $50, and "Night Life" sold for $150. However, in 1961, Patsy Cline made Willie's song, "Crazy" number one on the charts, a triumph followed by "Hello Walls," a song by Willie that Faron Young made number one.

By 1962, Willie and his second wife, Shirley Collie, together performed "Willingly" and "Touch Me." Both singles made the Top 10 and Willie's career was launched.

Even with success, Willie's generosity has been enormous. He is currently president of Farm Aid, Inc., putting on concerts and special benefits to aid farm families in trouble. As I say, he is truly a remarkable man.

Country Gravy

As Prepared by Willie Nelson

Ingredients:

1 Lb. Bacon
¼ Cup Flour
2 Cups Skim Milk
Salt to Taste
Pepper to Taste

Directions:

Fry bacon, remove from pan, leaving grease. Stir flour into grease, cook until browned. Slowly add skim milk, stirring to blend. Season to taste with salt and pepper. Simmer until thickened.

Serve over biscuits and eggs.

4 servings

Notes

Jim Varney

Jim Varney is the dumbest man on television. He tries; no one ever questions his efforts. He's like the next door neighbor who is determined to restore his house himself without knowledge or previous experience. The 350 piece tool kit he buys from Sears is guaranteed not to have the 3 tools he needed to put the new television antenna on the roof. The ladder he buys will either be too short or so long that he can not get it anchored to the ground. The dripping faucet will become a flood when he forgets to turn off the water. The leaky toilet . . . You get the idea. He's the guy down the block who's perpetually in the hospital emergency room, the nerdy kid with all the Band-Aids who went to your high school, the guy in the factory who means well, is a good worker, but don't ever let him think for himself.

Jim Varney is also one of the most versatile actors in show business. He has starred in Shakespeare's "Midsummer Night's Dream," in Arthur Miller's "Death Of A Salesman," in Harold Pinter's dramatic "The Homecoming," and numerous other productions ranging from "Guys & Dolls" to "Detective Story," to "A Funny Thing Happened On The Way to The Forum."

And Jim Varney is a singer and entertainer. He has appeared on "Pop Goes The Country," "Operation Petticoat," "Alice," the "Johnny Cash Special," the "Johnny Carson Special," and numerous others.

How can my description be so varied? It's because you probably know Jim for one of his characters, Ernest P. Worrell. Ernest P. Worrell has been described as "every-man's neighbor," the kind of person who never gets things quite right and never loses hope. He has been used in numerous commercials in the top 50 markets, an immensely successful vehicle for selling all manner of products.

As one media writer, Mike Price, commented in "Nashville" Magazine, "Ol' Ernest is so dumb everybody, anybody, can feel superior to him. Everybody knows an Ernest P. Worrell in his own life. There's an Ernest in every classroom of every school in the world. Yes, and also in every factory, business office, restaurant, sales meeting, lunchroom, locker room, car pool, service club, and community sing. Wherever, whenever, more than two people congregate, the one who's the biggest dispstick is your Ernest P. Worrell . . ."

Jim told me that he considers commercials an art form and I must say that I do, too. I get angry with actors who look upon commercials as being beneath them. They're an art form unto themselves. It takes a lot of skill to do a commercial. There is split second timing. You have to hold the product just the right way. Often you will have to do 40 takes, doing each of them with the same enthusiasm and excitement as though it were the first time.

A lot of people don't know what it takes to do commercials. It is also an excellent way for younger and older people to make some money and to gain exposure on television. And if you're a musical performer, it allows you to pay for a lot of musical arrangements and buy a lot of gowns.

I know that I feel very indebted to Wesson Oil and the other companies with which I have worked. They've paid a lot of my bills over the years. I am always as professional as possible, knowing that time is money when you're in the studio. I try to give them what they want in the shortest possible time. I also do a consumer update report for Pine Sol — two minute pieces of copy. It's quite a challenge for me and I will often try to do 30 or 40 at a time in less than 1½ hours, in an attempt to beat my own record of the most done in the shortest time. Of course, after I'm through my tongue doesn't work anymore!

Jim mentioned that he had a knife collection. I was never much of a collector until my ex-husband started me collecting perfume bottles from all over the world. As a result, I have a number of unusual items that are quite beautiful.

If you saw me "helping" Jim on my show, don't worry about the recipe. It is an excellent one and will taste delicious. I became a little overly enthusiastic with the corn starch, putting in more than Jim told me I should. As a result, the gravy I created was too thick. Well, actually, it was the consistency of concrete. When the recipe is followed correctly, it is a smooth, tasty, delightful gravy. I guess the moral is that if you invite me over for dinner and want to serve Jim's gravy, keep me in the living room. Don't invite me in your kitchen. Don't ask me to help with the preparation!

Curry Pepper Steak

As Prepared by Jim Varney

Ingredients:

2 Tbsp. Wesson Oil
2 Lbs. Steak, Cut into Strips
1 Onion, Cut into Strips
1 Tsp. Corn Starch
1 Tsp. Curry
1 Clove Garlic
1 Green & 1 Yellow Pepper
  (if possible) Cut into Strips
½ Cup Water
1½ Cups Uncooked Rice

Directions:

Cut steak into strips. Cut onions and peppers into strips. Saute meat in oil, add onion strips, then add corn starch and stir, cook until browned over low heat. Add curry, garlic, peppers, water and cover. Simmer over low heat until boiling.

Prepare rice according to directions on package, and serve meat mixture over rice.

4 servings

Notes

Irlene Mandrell

rlene Mandrell reminds me of a younger version of Goldie Hawn, the comedian/actress. She is the youngest of the Mandrell sisters, Barbara Mandrell being the best known of the three. She is also an extremely tiny woman, the pot she used to prepare her recipe on my show almost being bigger than she was. It was difficult for me to imagine the fact that she had given birth just 2½ months earlier.

The baby was born on Christmas day, a fact that delighted me. Both Barbara Mandrell and my own father had the day of Christ's birth as the day they were born and that always seems rather special to me. When I got to hold the infant on my show, I again realized how warm and wonderful each new life can be.

When Irlene became a musician, she chose an instrument few women select—the drums. However, her choice was a good one because she has become extremely skilled and successful. She was born in Corpus Christi, Texas, raised in California, then relocated to Nashville when she was a teenager. Her skill with the drums resulted in her becoming a player with the Do-Rites, her sister Barbara's band. By the time she was 16, she had traveled over 500,000 miles as a professional musician. When she reached 20, she had played in every major city in the United States, made appearances throughout Europe, and was considered one of the best drummers in Nashville.

Like Goldie Hawn, Irlene has both good looks and talent beyond that which made her well known. She has appeared on numerous television shows, including "The Tonight

Show," "The Today Show," "Love Boat," "Password Plus," "Nashville Now," and many others, including her own television special. Her work in commercials has included everything from being seductive in a mattress company

advertisement to being a tomboy auto mechanic for an auto supply chain, to being the "Go Bananas" girl for Cover Girl posters, television ads, and in Glamour Magazine. She has also been a regular on the series, "Hee Haw."

Her being a drummer has been so unusual that not everyone who sees Irlene recognizes who she is. She told me that when she first started, there were so few female drummers that there was quite a bit of confusion. When the sisters would play at fairs, people assumed that she was a long haired, hippie boy.

Fairs can be rough for all entertainers at best, though. Many a time I have had to make an appearance following a tractor race. And the flies the fairs attract are so big and numerous, you sometimes feel that you are on stage, fighting for your life as the flies buzz all around you.

While we were eating our salad after Irlene had finished cooking on the show, I remembered a rather humorous incident that occurred with a housekeeper who worked for me for a while. She had served the salad and I noticed something rather fuzzy on some of the lettuce. I thought it might be some new type of vegetable or special seasoning until I looked closer and realized that it appeared to be fibers of some kind. So I asked the housekeeper what it was. She said she had dropped the salad onto the carpet, but didn't want to waste it so she just picked it up and put it back in the bowl!

FOOD FACTS

There is more Vitamin B in rare beef than in beef that is well done.

●

The most nutritious natural vegetable food known, and the only true meat substitute (in the legume family) is — the soybean.

●

Did you know one of the oldest processed foods, prepared since 1000 B.C. in the Mediterranean is — sausage.

●

Less than 100 years ago, Rudolph Boysen grafted a raspberry, loganberry, and blackberry to create the first — boysenberry!

Steak Stew

As Prepared by Irlene Mandrell

Ingredients:

MARINADE:

*5 Cups Lean Rib-Eye Steak,
    Bite-Size Pieces*
1½ Cups Worcestershire Sauce
1 Cup Soy Sauce
1 Tbsp. Ginger Powder
Salt and Pepper to Taste

STEW:

1 Lb. Bag Carrots, Peeled
5 Potatoes
10 Cups Water
*2½ Bell Peppers, Cut into
    Bite-Size Pieces*
2 Cups Chopped Onion
1 Med. Can Corn
1 Med. Can Peas
1 Med. Can Green Beans
1 Cup Cauliflower
1 Cup Broccoli
2 Stalks Celery
1 Pkg. Sloppy Joe Mix
1 Tbsp. Salsa
3 15-Oz. Cans Tomato Sauce
2 Tbsp. Barbecue Sauce
1 Can Tomato Soup
Chili Powder to Taste
Salt and Pepper to Taste

Directions:

Add together Worcestershire sauce, soy sauce, ginger powder, salt and pepper. Marinate steak pieces in the mixture for several hours.

Cut carrots and potatoes into bite-sized chunks and steam. Add together water, carrots, potatoes, bell peppers, onion, corn, peas, green beans, cauliflower, broccoli, and celery. Add to vegetable mixture: marinated steak pieces, sloppy joe mix, salsa, tomato sauce, barbecue sauce, and tomato soup. Add chili powder, salt and pepper to taste. Simmer in a dutch oven as long as possible—the longer the better. (Minimum 1½ hours.)

*Vegetables can be Changed to Preparer's Taste

4-6 servings

Notes

The Bellamy Brothers

The music of the Bellamy Brothers is a different kind of country sound. Neither brother is comfortable with songs that tell of lost loves and the pain of life. Instead they produce tunes with such delightful titles as "If I Said You Had A Beautiful Body (Would You Hold It Against Me?)," "You're My Favorite Waste Of Time," and "I'd Lie to You For Your Love." As they explain, "It's fun music, as opposed to cheatin' and drinkin' songs. Our style is basically an up, feel-good side to country music. After all, our job is to make the *fans* happy.

Perhaps part of Howard and David's difference comes from the type of country that is their background. They are from rural Darby, Florida, an area where farming involves orange groves and cattle, not cotton, and the nearest big city is Tampa, quite a distance away.

The Bellamy Brothers became internationally known because of a song that was at the top of both the pop and the country charts called "Let Your Love Flow." Going to the top of the pop charts was not something they had anticipated.

In their earlier years, pop had been somewhat of an influence. They used to listen to works by The Beatles, Everly Brothers, and Van Morrison during their teen years, but their father was a musician who played western-swing and bluegrass. He had his own band, played at home, and used to take the family to Tampa where they saw soul, Rhythm & Blues, and rock artists.

The first song to make them famous was a country song written in 1971. Howard, the older of the two brothers, awakened one morning to find that a snake was in his bed. That rather unsettling experience led to the song "Spiders And Snakes" which Jim Stafford sang, taking it to the top of the country charts. Suddenly the brothers gained recognition well beyond Florida, though for a country sound. So it was quite a surprise to them when "Let Your Love Flow"

was such a solid cross-over and brought them an international audience for pop music. They went on a European tour and spent the better part of two years abroad. Europe became "our second home because they were so good to us," said David.

"If I Said You Had A Beautiful Body (Would You Hold It Against Me?)," a song that I think has one of the most delightful titles I've ever heard, took the brothers back to the country music charts. They received a Grammy nomination for the song in 1979 and quickly followed it with such releases as "Redneck Girl," "When I'm Away From You," and "Dancin' Cowboys," all successful country songs. It was a type of music that was their first love and they made a smooth transition from their pop music success to country where they are firmly entrenched today.

When I was talking with Howard and David, they mentioned basketball, an extremely important amateur and professional sport in the south and midwest. I used to love to play basketball along with other sports, which was probably a good thing. Being the youngest of 10 and always having several brothers around, I was elected to fill in for any position they needed in any game they were playing.

Being poor, our equipment was often improvised. Football was a game we played with a tin can. Many was the time when the tin can would be passed to me, I would start to run, then get tackled and have the wind knocked out of me. I was also a cheerleader, a fact that probably should have destroyed my singing voice. As a kid, I used to scream at the top of my lungs until I was so hoarse that I was unable to speak.

My sons are both songwriters and singers so I have seen how difficult writing can be. It is an extremely lonely task since it requires isolation to create. When you combine that with performing with someone close to you, it can become intense. Yet David and Howard not only work together, they live with their wives, children, sister, grandmother, and parents in five separate homes on the family farm in Darby. They also raise the odd combination of exotic game birds and a small herd of Brahman cattle. They say they have no trouble getting along, though I suspect that the separate homes help when normal tensions arise.

Actually, there are entertainers who envy David and Howard being on that farm. When you are alone in a strange hotel, the cities changing night after night, knowing that you have roots, a home and family waiting for you makes for an extremely comforting situation. There is a peace that would otherwise be lacking.

Stir-Fry Shrimp

As Prepared by The Bellamy Brothers

Ingredients:

2 Tbsp. Wesson Oil
3 Cloves Garlic (Minced)
1 Ginger Root (Chopped)
1 Med. White Onion (Chopped)
2 Lbs. Med. Shrimp
   (Cleaned and De-Veined)
½ Head Cabbage (Shredded)
1 Bunch Broccoli Flowerettes
1 Bell Pepper
   (Coarsely Chopped)
1 Yellow Onion (Chopped)
6-8 Scallions (Chopped)

Directions:

Break broccoli flowerettes and shred cabbage. Heat wok, add oil, garlic, ginger root, and white onion. Add shrimp, cook until pink. Remove all and set aside.

Saute cabbage, broccoli, bell pepper, yellow onion, and scallions in wok. Add first shrimp mixture back into wok. Heat all together. Serve over brown rice.

4 servings

Notes

Ricky Skaggs

t was ironic that my first guest on Country Kitchen would be Ricky Skaggs because our backgrounds were quite similar. We were both born in small towns. His birthplace was Cordell, Kentucky, and mine was in Dale, Indiana.

Music was in both of our lives as far back as either of us could remember. I remember singing for relatives when I was three years old, then passing the hat. Ricky was five when his father, Hobart Skaggs, showed him a few simple chords on the mandolin. Hobart was a construction worker who had to be away on a job for two weeks and, when he returned, Ricky had taught himself more complex playing. His father recognized that he was a prodigy and began teaching him music more seriously. As a result, Ricky can play the guitar, banjo, mandolin, fiddle, and such lesser known instruments as the telecaster (a 1950's version of the Fender guitar) and the mandocaster (a 5 stringed electric mandolin).

While Ricky's parents, Hobart and Dorothy Thompson Skaggs, are accomplished musicians in their own right, both having performed in churches and on Kentucky radio shows, Ricky's achievements have been unusual. From the moment he learned to play the mandolin, he began performing at fairs and town socials. He appeared on Lester Flatt and Earl Scruggs' Martha White-sponsored TV show when he was seven, performing "Ruby" and "Honky Tonk Swing," on his first professional appearance.

Ricky's career advanced steadily until, at 27, he achieved what he considers the highest honor of his life. In June, 1982, he became the 61st and youngest member of the Grand Ole Opry, a radio show that was my family's favorite when I was growing up.

I had always enjoyed Ricky's music and had seen him

winning his various awards on television. But the first time I met him was when we were both in a hotel restaurant at EPCOT Center in Florida. He was with his young son, Andrew, who kept staring at me throughout his meal. I smiled at him, but neither Ricky nor I wanted to bother the other while we were eating.

Afterwards Ricky came over to introduce his little boy, Andrew, and himself. He was extremely nice and polite, yet I had no idea that he would be my very first guest on Country Kitchen.

The true character of Ricky Skaggs was not evident until the day of that first show we did together. A dear friend of mine was with us for the taping, and early that morning he suffered a heart attack. I had to rush to the hospital with him, then call the producer to tell him what had happened while Ricky was at the studio, waiting.

Ricky was forced to wait for me for several hours because I refused to leave the hospital until I was certain he was going to be all right. Ricky is a man with an intense performing schedule that has kept him on the road as much as 300 days a year. Yet he never complained about having to wait, either to the staff or to me. When I finally did arrive, his only concern was for my friend. "Will he make it? Will he be all right? Is there anything I can do to help you?"

Ironically, during the planning for a future show involving his wife, Sharon White, a member of the White Family, I was called in the middle of the night before the day she was to appear. Ricky's son, Andrew, had been in a car with his mother when she had pulled out to pass a truck driver. The trucker was under the influence and, for some reason, became angry enough to pull a handgun and fire a shot at the car. Andrew was struck in the face and rushed to the hospital. Ricky and Sharon immediately rushed to be with him.

While there was irony in the circumstances surrounding both their appearances on my show, the second incident revealed a great deal about Ricky's character. Just a few days after Andrew was shot, a situation from which he fortunately fully recovered, Sharon told me that he completely forgave the man who did it. The idea that he would love enough to do something so selfless shows a great deal about the way in which he was raised.

That love is also obvious in Ricky's relationship with his wife, Sharon White. They are both entertainers and have an understanding of the pressures that are on a marriage when the partners must travel to earn their living. He explained that Sharon is his best friend and he feels that he is her best friend. They have developed a closeness that has made their marriage extremely successful.

For my show, Ricky prepared a country breakfast that is far more interesting than it sounds. The recipe is one he learned from his mother, but he is so serious about cooking that he brought his own skillet from home.

Is the breakfast good? I had spent the morning of the show at the hospital with my friend. When I knew my friend would be all right, I raced to the taping so I would not keep everyone waiting any longer than necessary. Since I hadn't eaten, I was hoping that Ricky's cooking would come close to his abilities as a musician. Fortunately, he is an excellent cook and the meal is delicious.

Country Breakfast

As Prepared by Ricky Skaggs

Ingredients:

2 Cups All-Purpose Flour
1 Tsp. Salt
2 Tsp. Pepper
2 Cups Whole Milk
Wesson Oil
Cornbread, 1 Sheet, 9x13,
   Precooked
6 Eggs
Biscuits, 1 Doz., Precooked
1½ Lbs. Fresh Pork Tenderloin,
   Sliced About ¼" to ½" Thick

Directions:

Mix flour, salt and pepper together. (Add more salt or pepper to taste). Dust tenderloin in flour mixture. Fry pieces of tenderloin in a little oil over medium heat until meat is as done as desired. Remove tenderloin from skillet.

Cut the bottom off of the cornbread you have prepared and cut it into 1″ squares. Cornbread should be crusty, not soft. Fry cornbread squares in the same oil as the meat, until they are browned, like croutons. Remove cornbread squares from oil.

Add leftover flour mixture to the oil, and heat, stirring until brown. Add whole milk to form a thick gravy, stirring. Add the squares of cornbread crust to the gravy and keep stirring until gravy achieves desired thickness.

Take eggs and fry sunny side up or over easy. Split the biscuits, place eggs, meat, and biscuits on a plate. Cover as much as you want with gravy, and serve!

2-3 servings

Notes

Dottie West

ottie West hardly seems old enough to be a true pioneer in the country music business, but with more than 25 years in the field, she was actually one of the first female success stories. She began at a time when the industry did not look favorably upon females. They were called "girl singers," being lumped together as a category instead of being taken seriously as individual, solo artists. She was one of the first to achieve headliner status, making the public aware that a talented woman could become just as popular as the males who then dominated the industry.

Dottie has always lived in the Nashville area, being raised in a poor family of ten, much like my own, near that music capital. She majored in music at Tennessee Tech then, oddly, began a country music career in Cleveland, Ohio. There she obtained her own country music television show, periodically returning to Nashville to try to obtain a recording contract as a performer. That contract came in 1959. Two years later she became a songwriter, developing friendships with other struggling new writer/singers such as Willie Nelson, Roger Miller, and Hank Cochran.

"Is This Me" became Dottie's first major hit song, a Jim Reeves rendition, taking it to the top of the charts in 1963. Eventually she would write more than 400 songs, obtaining several BMI awards for her work. She also began producing memorable, Clio Award winning music for television commercials. One, "Country Sunshine," written in 1973, became the immensely popular commercial jingle

for Coca-Cola. In fact, the song was so good that, unrelated to Coca-Cola, I have used it in my act.

Dottie and I have worked together in the past and I have always found her an extremely likeable person. We were on the big country music two-hour special of "The Love Boat" where she wore this gorgeous white cowgirl outfit, complete with guns. She also appeared with me on the annual United Cerebral Palsy Telethon which I do every year. During those periods I realized that she has gained some of her energy by knowing how to relax, taking any free moments to sit and rest.

Dottie was one of the best cooks I have had on my show and she seems to feel as I do, that there is a relationship between sharing good food and giving love. I have a doctor, a wonderful Italian woman named Elsie Giorgi, who says that if someone doesn't like good food and good wine, they're kind of stingy with their feelings and with giving love. When you come to Elsie's office for a check-up, she'll say, "Would you like something to eat? Would you like a banana? Would you like a bagel?" She seems to know just what you might like, a delightful woman and a good friend. She and Dottie are quite different in their careers, but that relationship between preparing good food and showing love is one I see in both women.

Dottie commented on her success, saying how when you like something, you're good at it. Actually, she has been lucky in that regard since it's not always the case that you're good at it just because you like it. However, when you like something, you will *try* to be good at it. You will work harder than you might otherwise, developing that drive which can lead to success.

Dottie's success as a songwriter, singer, and actress has been extensive. She was the lead in the touring company of "The Best Little Whorehouse In Texas" and made her first movie recently, a film called "Aurora" about extra-terrestrials in Texas. She has sung such hits as "Would You Hold it Against Me," "Paper Mansions," "Country Girl," and numerous others, as well as teaming with other singers. Many know such Dottie West/Kenny Rogers hits as "Every Time Two Fools Collide," "Anyone Who Isn't Me Tonight," "All I Ever Need Is You," "What Are We Doin' In Love," and others, both with Kenny and stars such as Jimmy Dean, Don Gibson, and Jim Reeves.

Dottie West was a delightful guest for my show.

Stuffed Bell Peppers

As Prepared by Dottie West

Ingredients:

6 Lg. Green Bell Peppers
1 Lb. Lean Ground Round
½ Cup Chopped Celery
½ Cup Chopped Onions
½ Cup Chopped Mushrooms
2 Tsp. Worcestershire Sauce
½ Cup Red Cooking Sherry
1½ Dash Garlic Powder
½ Tsp. Onion Salt
½ Tsp. Black Pepper
    (Med. Grind) or to Taste
1 Pkg. Brown Wild Rice,
    Precooked, 8 Oz.
1 Small Can Tomato Sauce,
    8 Oz.
1 Can Mushroom Soup,
    10¾ Oz.
¼ Cup Water
4 Slices Bacon, Cooked and
    Crumbled into Bits
Small Pkg. Cheddar Cheese,
    4 Oz., Grated
¼ Cup Sliced Fresh Mushrooms

Directions:

Preheat oven to 350°. Saute celery, onions, and mushrooms in butter. Add Worcestershire sauce, garlic powder, onion salt, pepper, and red cooking sherry. Add ground round, and stir until meat is browned. Add 1 pkg. brown wild rice, precooked, to all and mix.

Take the bell peppers and cut out insides. Fill them with meat mixture. Place them upright in a deep baking dish. Pour tomato sauce, mushroom soup and water around peppers. Sprinkle bacon bits and grated cheddar cheese onto tops of peppers. Add a little more black pepper on top of peppers, and sliced fresh mushrooms. Cover with foil and bake at 350° for 30 minutes.

4-6 servings

Notes

George Lindsey

George is an old friend of mine with whom I first worked in 1962 doing a show for Oldsmobile. At that time industrial shows were major show business presentations. We did musicals such as "Good News," "Wonderful Town," and others. They would be done in a Broadway theater with top choreographers, directors, and other personnel. They were sponsored by industrial companies, but were major productions reviewed by the media.

For one particular production of "Wonderful Town," I played Ruth, the role Rosalind Russell had created when the show first appeared on Broadway, and George played "The Wreck." Even then, early in his career, you could tell he was going to be a big star.

George's physical appearance has led him to be given the role of "bad guys" in numerous television shows when he first arrived in Hollywood in 1962. His first starring role was in the 1962 Joshua Logan film, *Ensign Pulver*. Then, in 1964, George met Andy Griffith, a fact that resulted in the creation of the character "Goober" which he played in both the "Andy Griffith Show" and "Mayberry RFD." He was co-star in both series for over seven years. Immediately afterward George happened to drop by the set of "Hee-Haw" in order to say hello to friends. The producer asked him to read a couple of lines, delighted in what he heard, and George has been a featured cast member ever since. He also wrote and sang sketches, did pratfalls, and one-liners.

It is interesting to note that the Andy Griffith Show has nurtured many other fine performers. One of the best known from that show, in addition to George, is Ron Howard. He grew up on that show, playing the role of "Opie." Then Ron followed a life-long ambition to direct, creating such highly successful films as *Splash* and *Cocoon*.

When George and I were talking, I asked him what kind of act he does. His reply was "A good one." In reality he sings, performs, and improvises comedy very well.

George was wearing a large diamond ring, an obvious result of his success. However, he told an old joke explaining how he paid for it. He said, "My mother-in-law died and left me some money to buy her a stone!"

George has done more than just entertain. He is a man with an unusually generous spirit who has been involved with many charities. However, the one group of needy people for whom he spends the most time is the mentally handicapped. He has raised more than a million dollars for Special Olympics, a program designed to give the handicapped a sense of achievement and ability through sports. For several years he has also held the annual George Lindsey Celebrity Golf Tournament in Montgomery, Alabama, a tournament that benefits the mentally retarded children throughout Alabama. He brings in actors, entertainers, professional athletes, and other celebrities for the event (George is also a former top athlete and member of the Alabama Sports Hall Of Fame). In addition, he helped raise $450,000 to build the George Lindsey Aquatic Center at the Alabama State Hospital for the Mentally Retarded.

George now travels 40 weeks of the year, though he jokes that he has only been able to hold two jobs — "Andy Griffith" and "Hee-Haw." He is an extremely successful, gentle, generous man.

FOOD FACTS

Did you know it takes 75,000 flowers to gather one pound of . . . saffron.

●

The 1985-6 Gallup Poll on eating out says the nation's #1 choice as dinner entre in fine restaurants is still steak.

●

Did you know that this spice comes from the bark of evergreen trees grown along the Malabar Coast — cinnamon.

●

It wasn't considered a food in the United States until the mid 1800's because it was thought to be poisonous — the tomato.

Barbecued Chicken

As Prepared by George Lindsey

Ingredients:

BARBECUED CHICKEN

*1 Chicken, Cut into
  Conventional Parts
1 Jar, 16 Oz., Raw Honey,
  No Comb
1 Jar, 18 Oz.,
  Hot Barbecue Sauce
1 Jar, 18 Oz.,
  Reg. Barbecue Sauce*

Directions:

Bake chicken parts in a large pan in 350° oven for approximately 40 minutes. Pour off residue. Pour raw honey over the chicken, still in pan. Mix 1 jar hot barbecue sauce and 1 jar regular barbecue sauce and pour the mixture over the chicken. Refrigerate overnight, turn to baste occasionally.

Barbecue, basting with honey/barbecue mixture from pan. Serve with cole slaw.

COLE SLAW

*½ Head Shredded Cabbage
½ Bell Pepper,
  Chopped Med. Fine
1 Cup Mayonnaise
½ Tsp. Pepper*

Shred ½ head of cabbage. Mix cabbage, mayonnaise, pepper and ½ chopped bell pepper.

4-6 servings

Notes

B.J. Thomas

B.J. Thomas is an extremely exciting singer with a long, successful career that includes five Grammy Awards, numerous gold records, and approximately 40 million record sales. When his song "Raindrops Keep Falling On My Head" (written by Hal David and Burt Bachrach) became number one on Billboard's pop chart, a position it held for 4 weeks in January of 1970, it took its place as one of the top 25 hits of the decade. From there, B.J.'s musical success continued with such works as "Everybody's Out Of Town," "Rock And Roll Lullaby," "(Hey Won't You Play) Another Somebody Done Somebody Wrong Song," and even "America Is" which became the official theme song used during the restoration project of the Statue of Liberty.

But if asked to characterize himself, B.J. Thomas says that he is a "survivor." That term is more important than most people realize and I admire anyone who is a survivor in any business.

My mother was a survivor. She was a woman who raised 10 children on a little farm with no running water, no electricity. It was a very difficult life, yet she loved every minute of it. She was 88 years old, still on a bowling team and playing bingo when she died.

B.J.'s musical background has a rather humorous side to it. He was born in Hugo, Oklahoma, (he was Billy Joe Thomas then) then moved around the country until his family finally settled in Rosenburg, Texas. There was a strong country and R&B background in the music to which he was exposed, his favorites including works by stars ranging from Little Richard to Hank Williams and Ernest Tubb.

His own singing began in a church choir at the age of 14. He also became a member of a high school band called The Triumphs which did well enough to record a hit song in the form of the Hank Williams tune, "I'm So Lonesome I Could Cry." According to B.J., it would not have mattered to his father what song he recorded so long as it was the right type of music. "My dad told me not to come back unless I recorded something country."

B.J., his wife, Gloria, and I share an interest that I feel is extremely important. This is the problem of battered and abused children. B.J. had had a rough upbringing and my own father, much as I loved him, was an alcoholic who could also cause us a lot of pain.

For several years I have belonged to a national organization, Child Help, U.S.A., concerned with this problem. It is one that people need to know exists. There are ways to help the neglected and abused children as well as their parents.

Gloria Thomas and some other song writers wrote a song that has helped public awareness of the issue as well. It is called "Broken Toys" and it relates some of the pain of being raised in this kind of environment.

What is sad is that parents who neglect or abuse their children do not realize that they are doing it. Often they were abused themselves and have no idea how to react in a positive manner to their children. What we try to do is break this chain of abuse by making them aware of more constructive ways to handle their children.

B.J. had an interesting point about his cooking. He puts a tablespoon full of Wesson Oil in his pasta in order to keep it from sticking together. It was a good point that people who love Italian food, as I do, should know about. Too often the pasta comes out in one big lump, a problem solved with B.J.'s approach.

When B.J. lifted the lid on the pasta, he mentioned that inhaling the steam was good for the voice. That is something many singers have learned. In fact, when I am singing and have a slight cold, I will often get into a hot shower, inhaling as much steam as possible, then gently vocalize in order to warm up my voice. I have also used steam for my children when they have been ill. Of course, there are more ways to make steam than by inhaling over the hot pasta pot. However, I'm not certain that most of the others are quite as pleasant.

The surprising part of pasta is that it is not particularly fattening, one of the reasons many entertainers eat a lot of it (B.J. mentioned having leftovers microwaved in the small oven that is kept on his touring bus). Pasta is a complex carbohydrate and it is the sauce, not the pasta itself, that can put the weight on you.

The other nice part of pasta is that you can use almost anything with it. My son, Joseph, makes his with a sauce of Tabasco and parmesan cheese, and it tastes delicious. Yet, however you make it, I think you will find the following recipe delicious.

Fettucini Alfredo

As Prepared by B.J. Thomas

Ingredients:

1 16-Oz. Pkg. Fettucini Noodles
1½ Cups Grated Parmesan
   Cheese (Med. Container)
2½ Cups Half & Half Cream
1 Stick Pure Butter (Softened)
Coarsely Ground Black Pepper
   (to Taste)
2 Egg Yolks

*OPTIONAL:

1 Garlic Clove,
   Cut in Half & Minced

Directions:

Cook noodles according to package directions (salt and 2 tbsp. oil may be added to boiling water before adding noodles).

While noodles cook, combine parmesan cheese, half & half, softened butter, and yolks in medium sauce pan. Stir over medium heat until ingredients are melted. Drain noodles, rinse in hot water, pour into serving bowl. Add Alfredo sauce, mix well. Add pepper and/or minced garlic to taste.

4 servings

Notes

Darrell Waltrip

Though I have never been a professional race car driver like my guest, Darrell Waltrip, I can relate to the qualities that have made him motorsports' all-time money winner. Darrell is a man who leaves nothing to chance, and checks the smallest details before he starts his car. In his case, that means checking the engine, the tires, checking under the car, anticipating the slightest problem that could occur. His is an attitude that those of us who have been fortunate enough to be successful as entertainers can also understand.

There are always support personnel available to you when you perform—people who can help you with your hair, your make-up, your lighting, your sound equipment. But, in reality, the true professional recognizes the personal responsibility involved with racing a car or putting on a show. An amateur might do something when the mood strikes, but the professional must go out regardless of how he or she feels at the moment. Thus, constant attention to detail before each performance, before each race, or before any activity is a trait that helps ensure success. And this same thought can keep us from harm.

Darrell explained that the stock car racing he does is not dangerous, and that he would not do it if there was a serious risk to it. The problems arise only if you fail to take responsibility and make all the checks that are necessary.

Darrell's background is a fascinating one. He came from Owensboro, Kentucky, the same home town as mine, but began his professional career in 1968 at the Nashville

Speedway, eventually earning a record 78 victories. Then, in 1972, he entered his first Grand National race under the United States Auto Club sanction. He was 21 years old, a rookie, and had beaten such names as Roger McCluskey, Gordon Johncock, and Al and Bobby Unser.

With that kind of start, I asked Darrell what he thought about men such as Paul Newman, the actor and race car driver who just won a victory at 61 years of age. I wondered if he thought that racing should have an age limit for the drivers. Darrell readily agreed there should be. I expected him to make some remark about how an older man or woman might have slower reflexes, weakened eyesight, or some other impairment that could endanger the drivers. Instead, he laughingly said he wanted the age limit so he could win more races than was possible when competing with older drivers who have so much more experience. He explained that as long as the reflexes, eyes, coordination, and other physical skills necessary for driving are sound, then there is no reason to quit.

I have always felt that way about show business. As long as you can perform effectively and not be so old and decrepit that you fall off the stage, then you should be on stage if that's where you want to be.

Look at George Burns, for example. He is in his 90's, and an inspiration to everyone. He makes movies, appears on television, and refused to sign a nightclub contract for more than 10 years because he wasn't certain the club would still be around when he surpassed the century mark! When George was asked why he dated younger women instead of those his own age, he replied, "I would date women my age, but there aren't any alive!" George even continues to break into new fields, having made his first country music album when he was in his 80's.

I, for one, hope that happens to me. When people ask me how long I'm going to work, I tell them until I am 95. It's a privilege to be allowed to go up on stage and entertain others.

Darrell was nowhere near his nineties when he was my guest, yet he had already experienced more victories than many other competitors, regardless of age. He had been America's Driver of the Year three times, won the Winston Cup 68 times, and earned more than $6.3-million in prize money by the time he appeared on my show. That was more money than any other driver in history.

I was impressed with the way Darrell handled himself on my show. He was completely relaxed, skilled in the kitchen, and constantly joking. I suspect his performance with the food he made was as carefully practiced as his driving. He was a delight to get to know.

Fish Florentine

As Prepared by Darrell Waltrip

Ingredients:

1½-2 Lbs. White Fish Fillets
3 10-Oz. Pkg. Frozen Chopped
   Spinach, Thawed, Drained
2 Cups Chicken Broth
3 Cloves Garlic, Minced
½ Stick Butter
2 Tsp. Thyme
4 Tbsp. Flour
½ Cup Parmesan Cheese

Directions:

Preheat oven to 350°. Saute minced garlic cloves in butter, add flour, blend to make paste. Gradually add chicken broth to make sauce.

Pour half sauce into rectangular baking dish, put thawed spinach on top, sprinkle thyme over spinach. Lay fish fillets on top of spinach. Salt and pepper to taste. Pour rest of sauce over fish. Sprinkle with parmesan cheese. Bake 30 minutes at 350° F.

4 servings

Notes

Tanya Tucker

nyone who heard Tanya Tucker sing at the start of her career knew what kind of woman she was by the sound of her music. She was older, had been through a number of broken romances and lost loves, her throaty voice filled with lusty passion about life. At least, that was the image. The reality was that she was 13 years old, a girl who instinctively understood how to deliver effective country music. The following year she made her first appearance on the Grand Ole Opry and success just kept coming.

Tanya has always had a sense of direction and purpose. She was eight years old when she told her father, Beau Tucker, that she wanted to be a country singer. Instead of laughing at a childhood fantasy, he took her seriously and set to work to help her achieve that end.

The family moved around a lot during those early years. Tanya was born in Seminole, a hamlet in West Texas, then was raised in Arizona, Utah, Nevada, and Tennessee. But it was in the town of Henderson, Nevada, where Tanya found success. Nashville producer Billy Sherrill heard a demo tape she had recorded, flew to Nevada, and signed her to a contract that led to her first single, "Delta Dawn," that shot to the Number One position on the country charts. Her album by the same name reached the Top Ten.

Prior to her being on my show, Tanya and I had worked together on a two-hour country western star special of "The Love Boat." I asked her then what it was like to have had that type of rigorous life.

Tanya explained that being a child performer was all right with her. "It was a wonderful time of my life. I had a wonderful childhood. Sherrill was forming me, but it was honest. He's a true person. He let me be myself and do what I wanted, but he also directed me." She added that

that life was also all that she knew during this period.

My feeling, having worked with a lot of child performers over the years, is that it is an incredibly difficult life. It is so hard for them to keep a sense of identity and just a sense of being a child.

I know that on "The Brady Bunch" the children had extremely caring parents and there was a positive experience. However, so many child actors have incredibly pushy parents. A lot of the parents never made it in show business themselves so they are going to make certain their children make it. As a result, I have very mixed feelings, even though I know that you often have to just let the child go out and try to see if he can make it, if that is what he wants.

I worked through most of my schooling as a maid and housekeeper. I was with a family that had four children where I cleaned their house, ironed, and cooked. To this day I don't like housework, but then it was a complete drudge, especially for a child who would rather be out playing.

One of my favorite jobs in high school was when I got to be a soda jerk at Ken's Bright Spot which was also the bus station. I used to give away a lot, giving a double dip to someone who wanted a single dip. They also had a juke box there, and the whole place was a dream come true because I could work after school and on weekends, making as much as $14 a week. I worked there about three summers and it was one of my favorite jobs, especially compared to feeling like a slave when I was keeping house for someone.

Today I have a wonderful housekeeper named Connie Ponce. She is from Guatemala and takes great pride in the way she cleans my home and prepares delicious meals for me. She has been with me a number of years and I have seen how hard she works, her willingness to do her job, and the quality of her work. She takes great pride in doing the work and doing it well. Actually, that may be the reason I hate the work. I didn't do it very well.

Tanya and I were both singers as children, she singing with her sister and I singing with my sister, Emily. Tanya won a lot of contests and I won a few, Emily's and my favorite number being, "Let The Rest Of The World Go By." However, Tanya was fortunate enough to have both perseverance and the circumstances where her father was able to take her around to knock on the doors of people who might let her sing professionally. She was willing to keep coming back when turned down until she was successful.

Today the business is harder. There are fewer places for young performers than there were when I was growing up and even when Tanya was starting in the business. That means there is more discouragement and I sometimes wonder what I should say to a younger performer. Do I tell the person not to work some other job, that you have to believe, have to follow that dream no matter what the hardship? That's what I think is important, yet how do you tell new performers to just hang on? At the same time, I believe that that is what you must do if you are eventually going to be successful.

When Tanya was on my show, she was gaining great popularity in the music business once again. She had had several major hits early in her career, then faded from the scene for a short while, then returned again. Her skills are such that I know she will have the staying power that will keep her before the public eye for many years to come.

Dorito Chip Salad

As Prepared by Tanya Tucker

Ingredients:

½ Head Lettuce
2 Med. Ripe Tomatoes
2 Avocados
1 Cup Longhorn Cheese
6 Green Onions
1 Cup Croutons
1 Small Can Black Olives
1 Can Kidney Beans with Juice
1 Can Garbanzo Beans,
    Strained
1 Bottle Catalina Dressing
1 Red Onion, Chopped
Doritos, Regular or Nacho
    Cheese, Crumbled

Directions:

Mix dressing: kidney beans with juice, garbanzo beans, Catalina dressing, and red onion. Set aside.

Tear lettuce into bite-size pieces, chop tomatoes, chop avocados, grate longhorn cheese, and chop green onions. Add lettuce, tomatoes, avocados, cheese, green onions, and drained black olives to salad bowl, toss.

Add dressing to salad and mix, then sprinkle croutons and Doritos on top.

4-6 servings

Notes

Ralph Emery

alph Emery is probably the most famous talk show host in America, a man whose popularity is greater than such names as Johnny Carson and Larry King. He hosts The Nashville Network's nightly prime time program "Nashville Now," and in addition, his radio program, "Goody's Presents Ralph Emery," debuted in September of 1986 on 340 stations. Ralph is someone whom I respect greatly. Plus, I think he's sexy! Thus, I was delighted to interview the man who has interviewed me and almost everyone of prominence in the music and entertainment business.

Ralph told me about the early days of his career when he worked with the great Tex Ritter. They were disc jockeys together, Tex being on the radio from Monday through Thursday, then traveling to make appearances on Friday, Saturday, and Sunday. Ralph said that on Mondays, Tex would usually be tired. While music was playing, he would often sit smoking his pipe, then fall asleep. Within a few seconds, the pipe still clenched between his teeth, Tex would exhale, sending hot ashes into his lap. The next few moments, comical for the observer though possibly painful for Tex, went something like this: Tex would leap out of his chair, desperately pat at his stomach and crotch to put out the smoldering ashes, then quickly try to compose himself to change the music or say something calmly on the air.

That came as quite a surprise to me because I knew of Tex Ritter in quite a different way. When I was growing up in Indiana and Kentucky, Saturday night meant that we

would all go to the Rio movie theater for the double feature — a western and a monster movie. The monster movie was something like *The Headless Ghost* or *The Mummy's Ghost* or *The Werewolf,* and the cowboy movie often starred Tex Ritter.

As an adult, I have worked with John and Tom Ritter, Tex's sons. John is a very fine actor and Tom is an attorney and has cerebral palsy. For the past several years I have worked with the Ritters as the East Coast hostess for the annual United Cerebral Palsy Telethon where Tom has appeared. I found it interesting how all our lives have intertwined in such unusual ways when Ralph talked about his early days working with Tex.

Ralph spends more time on the radio and television each day than any other entertainer. I asked him how he is able to do so much and he said it's because he never takes himself too seriously. He is a man completely at ease with his work, something that is difficult to do when you interview.

I think one of the reasons I am such a big fan of Ralph's is because there was a period in my life when I was a professional interviewer. Most people don't know that, for about a year, I was the "Today Show" girl with Dave Garroway. This was during the period when the show was still a relatively new phenomenon in this country and I was one of the first female interviewers on daytime television.

One of my assignments on "Today" was to interview a Japanese woman who had written a book on flower arranging. She was new to America, married to a pilot who had taught her English that included pilot talk. Everything was discussed in relation to a clock face, just as a pilot during war time might say, "Enemy aircraft coming in at 3 o'clock." As a result, her book discussed flower arranging by explaining that certain flowers might be grouped at 4 o'clock and another one would be straight up at 12 noon.

I was told that I would have 7 minutes for my interview, an extremely long period of time for television. Fortunately I was assured that she spoke fluent English and there would be no problem.

On the day of the interview, everything appeared ready. The woman was dressed in traditional Japanese clothing, her book and some flower arrangements were on the set. As the interview began, we both kneeled on the floor and I asked her the first of my carefully prepared questions. The woman made a sound much like a sigh, smiled, and bowed her head.

I asked my second question. The woman made the sound again, smiled, and bowed her head.

I asked my third question, my fourth, my fifth. Always the reaction was the same. Then I glanced at the director who signaled to me that I still had five minutes to go. That was when I knew I was in trouble.

Suddenly "flop sweat" appeared on my forehead. "Flop sweat" is a show business term indicating the type of nervous sweat that appears on your forehead when you know that you are in trouble. I was failing — a *flop* — and that was why I was sweating. The woman apparently did *not* speak English. She could not *understand* my questions much less answer them. And I still had five seemingly endless minutes to go.

I decided that since the book was there, I would show pictures of her work, ignoring the fact that she could not communicate in English. I pointed to one image and said, "Why don't you describe this for us?" Again she made the sound, smiled, and bowed her head.

Thinking fast, I described the picture, saying something like, "And here, at three o'clock, we have an arrangement using daffodils and unhusked pussy willows." Then I moved on to the next picture while the off camera crew laughed their heads off and I was a nervous wreck.

I thought of that story when I interviewed Ralph because we had our own embarrassing moment. Just as we started singing, "There's No Business Like Show Business," the rug that drapes the piano fell off. It was a minor slip-up but an ironic one for someone remembering her first major flop as an interviewer.

Cheeseburger Noodles

As Prepared by Ralph Emery

Ingredients:

1 Lb. Ground Chuck
1 Cup Chopped Celery
1 Small Can Tomato Paste
2-3 Cans Water
1 Cup American Cheese
 (Diced)
1 Cup Uncooked Egg Noodles
 (Medium)
½ Cup Sliced Ripe Olives
Salt to Taste
Pepper to Taste
Grated American Cheese for
 Garnish

Directions:

Brown ground chuck with chopped celery, simmer 10 minutes covered, drain grease. Add tomato paste, water, diced American cheese, uncooked egg noodles, sliced ripe olives, salt, pepper to taste and simmer covered until noodles are cooked, about 30 minutes. Garnish with extra grated American cheese.

Serve with peas, salad and crescent rolls.

2-4 servings

Notes

Don Gay

Don Gay is a remarkable man. Although seemingly slight of build, he has one of the most powerful set of shoulders I've ever seen, shoulders that help him control 1,500 to 2,200 pounds of bucking bull. At the time he appeared on my show, he was the eight-time world champion bull rider. Don competes in the most dangerous and unpredictable activity in professional rodeo.

"It's not a case of *whether* you're going to get hurt when you rodeo. It's a case of *when* and how bad," he explained.

I asked Don the reason for rodeo's continuing popularity. He said he felt it was because of the way other sports have developed, that the public was tired of seeing the megabucks big league professionals complaining because they're *only* making two-million dollars a year. "Rodeo's an individual sport," he said. "It's just man against the animal and it's good, all around family entertainment."

Don claims he got into bull riding because he's "too lazy to work, too scared to steal, so I might as well ride bulls." In reality, Don's family has long been involved with the sport, his father having produced the Mesquite, Texas Rodeo for the past 29 years. "I guess I just never had a chance to learn golf," Don says.

But Don has no illusions about the way he makes a living, competing in 150 rodeos a year. "It's a lot like the Christians and the lions . . . People don't really want to see you get hurt, but they'd like to see you *almost* get hurt. It's a tough way to make a living."

The bulls Don rides are mixed breeds and thousands of

dollars are spent determining which ones will be the most aggressive and effective for rodeo riding. He joked that the ones that don't make it will likely end up as hamburger for Texas Tacos such as the ones he cooked on the show.

The enjoyment of sports is something I share with Don. I love baseball and boxing, especially boxing. I am hoping to have Mike Tyson on my show. I know Mike and attended the fight where he unified the heavyweight title in Las

Vegas, becoming the only boxer to win all three divisions at the same time.

I think many entertainers enjoy boxing and similar sports because we can relate to the athletes. They have to develop their timing, their bodies, and the ability to handle the unexpected in very tight situations. When you walk on stage in a nightclub or concert, it's very much like facing a wild animal. Each audience is different. Each has its own personality. It's just you there, alone, to tame them, to excite them, to wake them up, to quiet them down. There seems to be a lot of similarity between sports and entertaining.

Don's enthusiasm was such that he reminded me of Mickey Rooney and Judy Garland in their old movies. He showed us how to make Texas Tacos with the same type of attitude that Mickey had when he'd tell Judy that they'd use the barn, put on a show, and save the family farm. The quality of that taco was actually so good that I think it was the best I have ever had anywhere.

FOOD FACTS

What spice comes from the bark of evergreen trees grown along the Malabar Coast? Cinnamon.

•

Did you know that "hors d'oeuvre," freely translated, means "outside the main works?"

•

Did you know the annual consumption of seafood per American has reached 14.5 lbs.?

•

What food first arrived in the New World with Columbus on his second voyage? Chickens!

Texas Tacos

As Prepared by Don Gay

Ingredients:

1 Lb. Ground Beef
Salt to Taste
1 16-Oz. Can Cut Tomatoes
1 Clove Minced Garlic
¼ Tsp. Oregano
½ Head Lettuce
10 Corn Tortillas
½ Cup Wesson Oil
1 Cup Cheese
1 Cup Picante (to Taste)
2 Tsp. Jalapenos

Directions:

Brown ground beef over medium heat. Salt to taste while cooking. Shred lettuce in food processor or with knife. Mash cut tomatoes or put into blender until they are small chunks. Add minced garlic and oregano to tomatoes. Add salt to taste.

Warm corn tortillas over medium heat in oil, turning until hot. In each tortilla, wrap some of: meat, tomato mixture, lettuce, cheese, jalapenos, and picante. Serve hot.

4-5 servings

Notes

Barry Williams

It's always nice when a "mother" can be proud of her "son." Barry Williams was always a nice boy when he played my son, Greg Brady, on "The Brady Bunch." When I had him on my show, I was delighted to discover what a nice man he has become.

When Barry started out on "The Brady Bunch," he was a cute little kid, much shorter than I was. he had a crush on me, and we spent a lot of time talking with each other.

I remember one Christmas show where we were supposed to be in church and I was up in front, singing a Christmas carol. I happened to look over at Barry and he was sitting there, these big tears rolling down his cheeks. He was deeply moved by the song, a very sensitive and sensible kid who always loved music.

There was another incident with Barry that I found rather touching. He wanted to see a singer who was appearing at the Ambassador Hotel and wanted to take me with him. However, he wasn't old enough to drive, so he arranged for his older brother to bring him to my hotel. Then I drove the two of us to the Ambassador where we had a delightful evening, Barry making certain that we had a good dinner and a table for the show. When it was over, we went back to my hotel where Barry's brother picked him up and took him home. It was a sweet gesture on his part and took a lot of courage for him to ask me.

Barry's first car was a Porsche for which he saved for a long time. It was an old car, not in the best of shape, but it was his first and a dream come true.

The day Barry could make the last payment, he was given time off from work at the studio to pick it up. Then, on his way back to work, it started raining.

California rains and California drivers are a little different from those in the rest of the country. The rain is generally intense, the roads becoming slick very quickly. Yet the drivers often do not realize the limitations of their cars, driving too fast for the condition of the road. When that occurs, an accident is inevitable.

That was the case with Barry. Some driver, coming up behind him, had not considered the highway conditions. He slammed on his brakes too hard, went sliding about, and smashed into the back of the Porsche. Barry returned, absolutely crushed by the damage to the car he had only been able to drive a few miles.

Barry has many interests and skills. He is an excellent cook, an excellent swimmer and surfer. But he also likes to get in a small boat and go out to see the whales off the California coast line. He told me that the whales come right up to the side, something that fascinates him.

I think that one of the reasons Barry and the other kids on the "Brady Bunch" turned out so well is because they have wonderful, caring parents. They were not the usual stage parents, pushing their children to fill some fantasy in the parents' lives. Instead they were level headed and kept their children in line, giving them love and support.

Barry surprised me by being so mature. He is an extremely eligible bachelor who also kept making a number of double entendres during the cooking segment on his show. I felt that as his former "mother," I should reprimand him. At the same time, he was discussing the romance of candle light and music as it affects the meal. It was odd to see him this way after having known him growing up.

Periodically, I was involved with Barry's career after "The Brady Bunch." One time, when my ex-husband was general business manager for the Broadway show, *Pippin,* he told me that Barry was going to audition for the national tour-ing company. The auditions were being held at a theater that happened to be the very first New York theater in which I worked when I was in the chorus of the show, *Wish You Were Here.* I found out when Barry's audition would take place and went back stage to see him.

Poor Barry was extremely nervous: the chance to be in the show was a major break for him. I happened to know the producer so I decided to break the ice for Barry. When his name was called, I went out on the stage and began singing and clowning around.

Suddenly the producer called out, "Florence, is that you?" I told him it was, then said, "I'd like to introduce you to my friend, my colleague, Barry Williams." He gave a great audition and he got the part — I went to see him in the show in Cleveland, Ohio. Boy, was I proud!

While he was on my show, we talked about the continuing success of "The Brady Bunch." When last I heard, it was the second most successful show in international syndication, only "I Love Lucy" being seen by more people.

Barry and I realized that one of the reasons for the success was the fact that it was obvious that we all cared a lot about each other, both on and off the screen. We had a great rapport that seemed to come through to the audience, and I was delighted to have him on the show.

Stuffed Cornish Game Hens

As Prepared by Barry Williams

Ingredients:

4 Cornish Game Hens,
   1-1½ Lbs. Each
1 Cup Butter
6 Oz. Package Long Grain
   & Wild Rice Mixture
½ Cup Diced Celery
1 5-Oz. Can Water Chestnuts,
   Sliced
1 3-Oz. Can Chopped
   Mushrooms, Drained
1 Tbsp. Soy Sauce
2 Cans Drained, Sliced
   Mushrooms
½ Cup Dry White Wine
Salt to Taste
Pepper to Taste
1 Tbsp. Chopped Parsley
(Toothpick & String)

Directions:

Rub birds inside and out with salt and refrigerate several hours. Cook rice according to package, let cool. Preheat oven to 325° F. Combine diced celery, sliced water chestnuts, mushroom pieces, ¼ cup melted butter, soy sauce with cooked rice and toss lightly. Stuff birds.

Take ¼ cup melted butter and brush over outside of birds. Place birds in pan with legs up. Cover cavity with loose skin, secure with toothpick, and tie legs together with string. Bake for 1 hour and 15 minutes at 325° F., basting once or twice with drippings.

To prepare sauce: Saute 2 cans drained sliced mushrooms in ½ cup butter, dry white wine, pan drippings, and salt & pepper to taste. Pour sauce over birds to serve, top with chopped parsley. Serve with steamed vegetables.

4 servings

Notes

Larry Gatlin

arry Gatlin is so young looking, it is hard to imagine that he has been singing professionally for more than 30 years. Of course, the fact that he started when he was six years old may explain some of it. He, along with his brothers Steve, then four, and Rudy, then age two, first performed in the "Cavalcade of Talent" show at Hardin Simmons University in Abilene, Texas. Later they appeared on a Sunday morning radio program on a local station, this time getting paid — *10 cents each per week*.

It would seem that success was instant for Larry, a true poet whose songs have been recorded by stars as varied as Elvis Presley, the Carpenters, Barbra Streisand, Dottie West, Roy Clark, Hank Snow, Johnny Cash, and numerous others. In reality, he had to work in a variety of jobs to make ends meet. Separate from the music business, he once worked as a roofer, a bricklayer, an oil field laborer, and a janitor at WLAC TV in Nashville.

Today the Gatlin Brothers have a wonderful nightclub act. They are extremely successful, Larry having risen above a severe alcohol and drug problem to get his life together.

Larry was talking about the soup he was making and commented that "it tastes so good, your tongue will flap your brains out trying to get to it." It was a comment that reminded me of an old radio preacher I heard when I was a little girl. There was a woman who had become angry with him for something he had said, sending an extremely nasty letter to him. He mentioned the situation on the air, and then, referring to her tongue lashing, he said, "Now that's a

woman who can probably lick a skillet in the kitchen . . . while standing in the living room."

There is a sensitivity about Larry and the Gatlin Bothers that comes not only from Larry's conquering his personal problems but also from their caring about others. For example, they have produced a dramatic music video called "Runaway Go Home" on the problems of teenaged runaways.

The 5½ minute video began after the brothers learned about Oasis Center, Nashville's home for runaways which works to either return teenagers to their homes or, when their family is not the best place for them, to a loving foster home. Larry wrote the song, his initial inspiration coming when he was in Joliet, Illinois, and became lost. While looking for landmarks, he saw a billboard with the message, "Runaway, go home free on Trailways."

Larry wrote the song, and they decided to do the video. They used four teenagers who had lived on the streets before going to Oasis Center as some of the actors. The video shows the boys and girls at a truck stop, then becoming involved with everything from prostitution to shop lifting. Although the video shows one boy happily reunited with his father, the reality is that such endings are not always possible. Many times the children are on the streets for the very reason that going home is not possible. The parents are abusive, perhaps alcoholic and/or drug addicted. However, Oasis Center and similar organizations recognize this and work to get the teens into an environment that will be positive for them.

For quite a while, Larry made "Runaway Go Home" part of his act, singing it without explanation. As he commented, "I can't change the world and I don't presume to—I can barely take care of Larry 24 hours a day. I'll sing the song every night and if people ask me, I'll tell them about the situation."

FOOD FACTS

Celery seeds are so small, it takes over 750,000 to make a pound.

•

Did you know — there are over 100 varieties of the avocado.

•

Did you know sourdoughs appear in Egyptian records as early as 4000 B.C.?

•

The leading contender in the vegetable-used-as-fruit category is — rhubarb.

•

There are over 1,000 varieties of this fruit grown in North America . . . the apple.

Tortilla Soup

As Prepared by Larry Gatlin

Ingredients:

BROTH:

1 Whole Chicken
½ Onion
1 Clove Garlic
2-3 Bouillon Cubes

SOUP:

Wesson Oil
2 Pkgs. Corn Tortillas (20),
  Cut into 1 Inch Strips
1 Bell Pepper, Chopped Coarsely
1 Onion, Chopped Coarsely
3 Garlic Cloves, Chopped
1 Can Stewed Tomatoes, Cut Up
1 Can Garbanzo Beans
1 Tbsp. Chili Powder
2 Tbsp. Cumin
Salt to Taste
1-2 Cans Chicken Broth
  (may be needed)

Directions:

Place whole chicken in pot, cover with water, add onion, garlic, and bouillon cubes. Cook on medium heat until tender, reserve broth. Cut chicken into bite size pieces. In skillet, fry tortilla strips in 1 inch of oil and set aside. Pour off all but 3-4 tbsp. oil. Brown bell pepper, onion and garlic cloves in reserved oil. Add stewed tomatoes, chili powder, cumin, garbanzo beans, and salt. Add this to broth and chicken pieces. (You may need to add 1-2 cans of clear chicken broth at this point if soup is too thick.) Simmer until hot; 8-10 minutes. Serve with tortilla strips.

4-6 servings

Notes

Jim Nabors

Jim Nabors, one of my dearest friends, is an extremely sophisticated gentleman. His deep southern accent belies the rich singing voice that has delighted audiences across the continent.

I remember a time we were in Massachusetts doing a tent show together. The way we worked, we would alternate our acts and then close with a set together. Jim came out and did his 15 minutes, then I came out. I came to a very serious ballad and noticed the audience was distracted. They were fidgeting in their seats, whispering, and pointing over my head. I looked up and saw this bird that had somehow gotten under the tent. As I watched it circled for a few moments, then flew directly at my *crotch*!

I dropped the microphone, stopped singing and grabbed myself. As the audience screamed with laughter, the bird flew into the orchestra pit.

Slowly, composing myself, I picked up the mike, turned toward the now resting bird, and said, "Okay. Please, stay there." And then as an afterthought, "unless of course, you hear something you don't like."

Apparently the bird approved the rest of my act because it stayed where it was and, until later, I totally forgot it was in the orchestra pit. Then Jim came out to open the next set. He began singing a delightfully upbeat number when suddenly the bird flew out of the orchestra pit and right out of the tent.

Well, the audience, remembering that I had told the bird it could stay until it heard something it didn't like, went crazy. They imagined the bird actually decided it didn't like Jim's beginning and flew away. Poor Jim had *no idea* what had happened, and could only watch the audience laugh for several minutes.

Despite the fiasco with the bird, Jim enjoys an extremely successful career in show business, both as a singer and in comedy. Remember his Gomer Pyle character? However, unlike the bird attack from which he gracefully recovered, his first professional appearance in Los Angeles was a disaster. He had been raised in Alabama, then made his way to the west coast by working odd jobs in various cities. Someone knew he had a beautiful voice and hired him to sing at an extremely fancy wedding. The fee was $25 and the idea of a professional appearance made him nervous.

Jim went to the wedding in a rented tux, accompanied by his sister. Once there he discovered it was a candlelight service where they cut out all the lights, including the ones leading to the choir loft where he would be singing. The results of this arrangement seemed delightful . . . at first.

As Jim told me, "I crawled up to the choir loft, opened the door, and it was pitch black. I groped around in the dark, finally found a chair and sat down. Then the mothers of the bride and groom were seated, so I stood up to sing.

"There was a big congregation of people out there and I felt nervous and inexperienced, but I boomed forth with 'Ah, sweet mystery of life at last I found you . . .'

"You know how when you're nervous you move around without noticing where you're going? Well, I put my hands together and took a step forward as I was singing. And suddenly the floor fell out from beneath me. I'd stepped into the stairwell to the basement and just vanished.

"I fell a whole flight of stairs and all I could hear was this woman playing the organ. Well, I must have passed out for a couple of seconds, and when I came to, I felt like I was in the Twilight Zone.

"Nobody knew what had happened to me. So, when I crawled back up the stairs, and reappeared through a little velvet curtain outside the choir loft, the whole congregation applauded!

"Now my sister who never thought I was particularly funny, asked me, 'What were you doing?'

"I said, 'I fell and it wasn't funny.' "

"And she said, 'Maybe it wasn't, but the bride was *still* laughing when they came down the aisle.' "

Jim has now moved to Hawaii where he has a home on Diamond Head, a home so beautiful it has been written up in "Architectural Digest." I remember that right after doing "The Bells Are Ringing" in the Dorothy Chandler Pavilion in Los Angeles, I was so exhausted that Jim invited me to be his guest. I accepted and it was one of the most relaxing, delightful times I have spent anywhere. In fact, I was going to stay a week, and ended up staying two weeks. He showed me his ranch on Maui, an area that looks like Paradise, and the macadamia nut trees he grows.

Those macadamia nut trees led to a rather funny incident during one of his shows. Jim has a humorous number during which he invites a member of the audience up on stage with him. He asked one lady what she did for a living and she said that she sold barns. He commented that selling barns was an unusual occupation.

To Jim's astonishment, the woman replied, "Yes, but I'd love to sell you a barn because I'd just love to have your nuts in my barn." Once again the audience went wild.

Chinese Chicken Salad
As Prepared by Jim Nabors

Ingredients:

DRESSING

¾ Cup Apple Cider Vinegar
½ Cup Sugar
1 Cup Sesame Seed Oil (or
   Comb. Sesame Seed And
   Wesson Oil)
4 Tsp. Soy Sauce
2 Tsp. Toasted Sesame Seeds
Salt to Taste

SALAD

White Wine
6-9 Boneless Chicken Breasts
   (1-1½ per person)
4 Stalks Green Onions, Chopped
1 5-Oz. Can Water Chestnuts,
   Drained, Sliced
1 Med. Head Iceberg Lettuce, Torn
   into Bite Size Pieces
1 Med. Head Romaine Lettuce,
   Torn into Bite Size Pieces
6 Oz. Bean Sprouts
1 Bunch Chinese Parsley (May
   Substitute Coriander)
(Save a Few Sprigs for
   Garnish, Remove Leaves
   from Stems on Rest)
6 Oz. Wonton Skins, Cut into
   ¼ Inch Strips (Save Some for Sprinkling on Top of Salad)

Directions:

Mix cider vinegar, sugar, sesame seed oil, soy sauce, sesame seeds and salt together thoroughly; set aside.

Poach chicken breasts in equal parts water and white wine. Chop green onions, slice water chestnuts. Remove the skin from poached chicken and cut chicken into bite size pieces. Mix chicken, water chestnuts and green onions; marinate in just enough dressing to cover. Deep fry the wonton strips.

Just before serving, toss together iceberg lettuce, romaine lettuce, bean sprouts, chinese parsley, and all but a few of the wonton strips. Place mixture on a large platter or bowl. Place marinated chicken on top of lettuce. Sprinkle remaining wonton strips on top and garnish with several sprigs of chinese parsley.

6-8 servings

Notes

Jeannie C. Riley

I suspect that everyone in the world knows Jeannie C. Riley from her big hit, the Tom T. Hall song, "Harper Valley PTA." It was the story of a woman who was tired of being criticized by the community for a lifestyle which was outside of their accepted standards. It created an image of a woman who was brash, independent, different, yet with very positive standards.

The longevity of the song I suspect surprised everyone. Perhaps it was because so many people can relate to such an experience. Or perhaps it was because of the television show, "Harper Valley PTA," which starred Barbara Eden as the independent woman.

A hit such as the one Jeannie had can create as much of an image problem as a show that runs for a long period of time. There is a tendency to mistake the person for the role or, as in this case, the character implied by the song. Jeannie said that when people met her, they expected her to be the brassy, sassy mother who told off the community when, in reality, she is quite different.

People have a tendency in this country to want you to be the last character you played. This is a real problem if you played a villain, but I know that there are many who would like me to be Carol Brady the rest of my life. Yet I could not go on being Carol Brady. I think I have more depth and ability than that.

In fact, with a television series, the time you have while you are actually on the air to tell a story is so short that there is seldom great substance to the character. The cast of "The Brady Bunch" was all so close, so genuinely caring about each other, at least there was a sense of warmth projected during the shows. Yet there is always enough superficiality in the story lines caused by the limited time periods that there is a tendency to read traits into the cast that may or may not be there. When someone mentions Carol Brady, his or her memories from watching the program may involve a very different person than someone else imagines. Fortunately, I have been lucky that all the perceptions have been positive and that people have enjoyed that work so much. Now, I look for opportunities to give to an audience in as many ways as my talents allow, not just as Carol Brady. And that was the problem that Jeannie C. Riley faced after the success of "Harper Valley PTA."

Jeannie's daughter travels with her frequently, acting as a back-up singer. I remember one time when I did a night club act that included my four children and it was one of my happiest times on the road. I could have them with me all the time and they were all extremely professional. We normally spend so much time separated from our children that it is a wonderful feeling when they have the talent and interest to accompany us.

Jeannie has been married twice, both times to the same man. She said that she became involved with other men, yet each time that she was close enough to marry some other person after her divorce, there were what she called "spiritual roadblocks." It was only after she got back with her husband, remarrying him with a much deeper commitment, that she truly felt at peace.

FOOD FACTS

To make up one pound in weight, it takes over 1,000 cloves.

•

Plum Pudding contains only raisins and currants — and no plums!

•

Did you know America's favorite vegetable is corn?

•

Garlic contains a natural antibiotic and can cure insect bites as well as bronchial complaints.

•

20% of the 525 pounds of food annually consumed by the typical American is — sugar.

Texas Hot Tamale Pie

As Prepared by Jeannie C. Riley

Ingredients:

*1 Lg. Onion
1 Bell Pepper
1 Stalk Celery
2 Tbsp. Wesson Oil
2 Lbs. Lean Ground Beef
1 Tsp. Salt
2 Tbsp. Gebhardt's
    Chili Seasoning Mix
1 8-Oz. Can Hunt's
    Tomato Sauce
1 8-10 Oz. Pkg. Corn
    Muffin Mix (Instant)
1 Cup Evaporated Milk
1 Small Package Sharp Cheese*

Directions:

Preheat oven to 400° F. Coarsely chop onion, bell pepper, celery. Cook vegetables in oil until tender.

While vegetables are cooking, brown beef and salt in another pan. Drain beef. Add chili seasoning mix and tomato sauce to beef, add a small amount of water if mixture is too dry.

Add vegetables to meat mixture. Simmer for 5 minutes.

Place cooked mixture in a large casserole. Mix corn muffin mix and evaporated milk in a small mixing bowl, pour over meat.

Grate cheese to liberally cover top of corn muffin mixture. Bake in 400° oven for about 20 minutes, or until nicely brown on top.

6-8 servings

Notes

Richard Sterban

When Richard Sterban was my guest on Country Kitchen, I discovered that the singing we did in childhood was quite the opposite of our present styles. Richard, a long time member of the world famous Oak Ridge Boys, is known for his deep bass voice. However, his earliest singing, including a Sunday School solo at the age of seven, was as a soprano. His range did not reach the lower register until he was in high school.

I was quite the opposite. I was born with a full range voice and such a love of singing that as my mother told me, I knew fifty songs when I was two years old.

There were 10 of us children attending parochial school when we were growing up, I being the youngest. When the nuns discovered that I could sing, I was placed in the church choir, moving over to the adult choir by the time I was in the third grade. There I learned to sing the old Latin masses, beautiful works that have for centuries been a part of the church's musical heritage.

The adult choir in which I was singing was not that large and we could not spare certain voices. There were occasional Saturday nights when the tenor or the bass would have a little too much to drink, then be unable to sing the next day. When that occurred, I was pressed into service to sing whichever part was necessary. My current soprano voice, the opposite of Richard's deep bass, was preceded in school by a range that included bass, tenor, alto, and soprano.

At the time I was singing such a broad range, I never thought anything of it. We were singing Gregorian chant and I did whatever the Sister wanted. However, I now realize that it was the best training a young singer could have. I learned to use the full range of my voice, developing the depth that I have today. (My family might tell you that additional training came just from being the youngest of ten children and having to scream to be heard.)

Richard and I joked about his appearance. He is the shortest of the Oak Ridge boys and extremely thin, yet people always expect such a deep bass voice to emanate only from an extremely big man.

I, too, was quite tiny when I sang as a child, though part of my problem came as a result of my brother, Tommy. I love him dearly today, but when we were growing up, he delighted in tricking me out of his favorite food. On those rare occasions when we could afford fried chicken, he would whisper to me that if I ate the wing, I would grow another arm, and if I ate the leg, I would grow another leg. Naturally, I believed him and, frightened of looking so strange, I passed the chicken to him. He always managed to "save me" from peril.

The recipe Richard prepared on the show was lasagna, a dish his mother taught him how to cook in her "magic pot." The "magic pot" is something I long ago discovered existed in certain ethnic — Italian or Greek — families. No matter how many people happen to drop over for a visit, there is always enough food to be shared by everyone.

I remember when I got married and lived in New York, our best friends lived with their family in a huge house in Brooklyn. They were Italian and any number of people were likely to just drop by. Always there was lasagna or some other dish on the stove and always there was more than enough for everyone, no matter how many people happened to come over unexpectedly. I talk about their "magic pot," but the reality is that that trait, the willingness to share, reflects a warm and generous spirit I greatly admire.

As well, Richard is a man who takes great pride in his appearance. Many male performers in the country music field feel that being personally comfortable is their primary concern. They will go on stage in a T-shirt and jeans or other casual clothing. But Richard is likely to be in a three piece suit. In fact, he once hired Peter O'Brien, a men's fashion consultant and former editor of Gentleman's Quarterly, now GQ Magazine, to teach him how to look his best.

I admire this trait in Richard because I also feel that you should look your best when performing. I see going out on stage as second only to going to church. People want to see you at your best. It's part of the theatrics and it's a sign of respect for the audience when you respond accordingly. I found his pride in the way he looks when he goes on stage refreshing.

Lasagna

As Prepared by Richard Sterban

Ingredients:

3 Tbsp. Olive Oil or Wesson Oil
1 Small Onion
1 Clove Garlic, Minced
1½ Lbs. Ground Beef
3 10-Oz. Cans Tomato Puree
2 6-Oz. Cans Tomato Paste
2 6-Oz. Cans Water
1 Tsp. Salt
½ Tsp. Black Pepper
½ Tsp. Oregano
¼ Tsp. Sugar
1 Lb. Lasagna Noodles
1 Tsp. Wesson Oil
1 Tsp. Salt
*1 Lb. Ricotta Cheese or Cottage
  Cheese*
*8 Oz. Mozzarella Cheese, Sliced
  Thinly*
4 Eggs, Hard Boiled (Optional)
½ Cup Grated Parmesan Cheese

Directions:

In large pan on medium heat, brown chopped onion and minced garlic in olive oil. Add ground beef, cook until brown and crumbly. Stir in tomato puree, tomato paste, water, 1 tsp. salt, black pepper, oregano, and sugar. Cover, simmer about 1½ hours.

Cook lasagna noodles in 6 quarts boiling water with 1 tsp. salt and salad oil. Cook 15 minutes, drain, run under cold water.

Preheat oven to 350°.

In a 9 X 13 pan, spread a thin layer of tomato sauce, then noodles, more sauce, ricotta cheese, mozzarella cheese, and hard-boiled eggs, and sauce again. Repeat until noodles are gone, about 3 layers, (top layer is tomato sauce and ½ cup parmesan cheese.) Bake at 350° for about 45 minutes, covered.

12 servings

Notes

Minnie Pearl

f all the people I have met in every phase of show business, one of the nicest is Minnie Pearl. What most people do not realize is that Minnie Pearl is actually Sarah Ophelia Cannon, a remarkable woman who has been married to Henry Cannon for more than 40 years. Theirs is an extremely close relationship, her husband acting as a business manager as well as being a pilot who flies her to her various concert engagements.

Minnie Pearl is one of those remarkable people who likes to help others entering show business. She tries to explain the harsh realities of the business, the fleeting nature of fame and money. She works to help them maintain their perspective.

What few people realize is that Minnie is an extremely intelligent woman. She and Mary Martin, another great star and a treasured friend of mine, both attended the exclusive Ward Belmont School.

Minnie Pearl was born during the Depression. As she explains, "I had a job for six years traveling from small town to small town in the South putting on amateur musical comedies for church and civic groups. It was a big thing at the time. There were hundreds of people doing that kind of work. To help publicize the amateur show I was directing in each town, I would appear before the Lion's Club and other luncheon groups. In return for their letting me announce my show, I'd do a couple minutes of entertainment for them. I'd do an interpretation of a country girl, Minnie Pearl, who was sort of a composite of the many I had met and seen. After I created her I named her Minnie Pearl after two fine old country names I loved."

Over the years, Minnie Pearl has evolved into a district character. Sarah Ophelia Cannon describes her as "uncomplicated. She's apple pie and clothes dried in the sun and the smell of fresh bread baking. I don't think people think of her so much as a show business act as just a friend. When I'm on stage, I'm just plain Minnie Pearl wearing my battered old straw hat and battered shoes. The price tag on my hat seems to be symbolic of all human frailty. There's old Minnie Pearl standing on stage in her best dress, telling everyone how proud she is to be there and she's forgotten to take the $1.98 price tag off her hat."

Minnie told me that she did not cook because her family was more successful than many and had servants who didn't want her in the kitchen. Since marrying, she has had the same housekeeper, who has been wonderful to her and her husband, Henry. Incidentally, the housekeeper's name is Mary Cannon — no relation, just a coincidence.

Minnie now has a museum in Nashville and tries to be there to show people around whenever she can. My sister, Marty, and her family visited the museum and told Minnie who she was. Minnie went out of her way to show them around, have pictures taken with them, and sign autographs. Yet it was something that just came naturally, a warm and generous spirit.

The Minnie Pearl character and her stories evolved from Ophelia's love of people and her observations of them. In her early years, when she was traveling from small town to small town with the theatrical acts, she would watch the people.

As she explained. "One of the rules of our company in Atlanta was that the local organization sponsoring the play would provide lodging for me. This meant I stayed with dozens of families in different small towns. I came from a happy family, but when I was working and staying with other families, I noticed how people were lonely and looking for some laughter. I also heard lots of country stories and songs. I'd encourage people to tell me stories. I'd file them in my mind. Every time I'd get in a crowd, I would tell those stories informally."

Eventually Minnie became a regular on the Grand Ole Opry. "Being on the Opry opened a new life for me. I was young. I would flirt with the audience, really ham it up to get extra encores. Though my father always used to listen to the Opry, I didn't know too much about the singers until I began to love the music. I've loved it ever since. There have been so many great people on the Opry — people like Roy Acuff, Tex Ritter, Red Foley, Ernest Tubb, Rod Brasfield, and Hank Williams — just too many to name. Today there are a lot of new singers and songwriters."

Minnie is now in her 70's, and in recent years has had a tough time with her health. She has had surgery and had to slow down to some degree. I sent her a get well card recently and she wrote back saying "thanks for taking the time." She is courageous in adversity and a positive inspiration to us all.

Minnie is having so much fun giving to others, she is thrilled to keep performing. As she said in her autobiography, "I'm not versatile like Carol Burnett or a Sammy Davis, Jr. All I have is Minnie Pearl. The Lord is good to me. He let me have her. He let me re-create her for these thousands of people for 40 years. She is always 'just so proud to be here!'."

And we're so proud to know Sarah Ophelia Cannon!

Creole Egg Casserole

As Prepared by Minnie Pearl

Ingredients:

*10 Hardboiled Eggs,
   Peeled, Sliced Thin
2 Cups Milk
1 Lg. Can Tomatoes
   (Undrained)
1 Lg. Onion, Chopped
1 Lg. Green Pepper, Chopped
1 Celery Rib, Chopped
2 Tbsp. Wesson Oil
Parmesan Cheese
4 Tbsp. Butter
5 Tbsp. Flour
Salt
Pepper
Worcestershire Sauce
Bitters
Lemon Pepper
Seasoned Salt*

Directions:

Preheat oven to 300°. Hardboil 10 eggs, peel and slice thin. In oil, saute chopped green pepper, celery rib, and onion until limp, (a few minutes). Add tomatoes, undrained, to this mixture, simmer covered for about 20 minutes.

Melt butter over low heat. Add flour and stir to blend. Add milk gradually, stirring continuously to make a thick paste. Add salt, pepper, Worcestershire sauce, bitters, lemon pepper, and seasoned salt to taste.

Layer a casserole dish with eggs, white sauce, parmesan cheese, then more layers in the same order until the dish is full, (finishing with parmesan cheese or croutons lightly buttered). Heat casserole at 300° until it is bubbly, for about 20 minutes.

4 servings

Notes

Robert Reed

It was a great pleasure to have Bob on my show because, for five years, he was one of my "husbands." That was the period when he was Mike Brady, the father of "The Brady Bunch," and I played his wife. However, the time we spent on the set was probably more concentrated than real married couples spend together in three times that period.

Later, Bob and I did ten variety hours and another ten episodes of "The Brady Brides." Overall we had an excellent relationship, though with occasional artistic squabbles. He cares so much about what he does that he is a constant perfectionist with his work. He even directed a few of our shows, a difficult task when the cast includes 9 regulars.

Bob frequently joked about our intimate relationship on "The Brady Bunch." The show would usually end with us in bed, me wearing a sexy nightgown and Bob in his pajamas. He would keep asking why it couldn't be for real, teasing me in front of the crew. After all, we were the first "TV Couple" to sleep in the same bed.

The one thing most people didn't realize was how tall Bob is. He is approximately 6'5", a little over a foot taller than I am. On "The Brady Bunch" every time we had to do a "two shot" — a close-up of the two of us together — Bob would squat down so he would look shorter. Otherwise the camera could not focus on both of us at the same time.

Bob is the divorced father of a daughter with whom he had not been able to spend much time since she lived with her mother. He missed the child and delighted in working with the kids on "The Brady Bunch," constantly trying to find things that would be educational and exciting for them. For example, one year he took all of them to Europe at his own expense, something I thought was incredibly generous. He also took all of us, and our families, on a fishing trip.

The fishing trip began at Paramount Pictures where we boarded a massive bus, coffee and doughnuts being served as we drove to Laguna. There we boarded a deep sea fishing boat and went out to sea. I was delighted that my little girl, Lizzie, won the prize for the most fish caught — approximately 30 sea bass.

Bob had a huge mansion in Pasadena where he held lavish parties. Oddly, within the entry way, there was a goldfish pond left over from the original builders. The pond should have been obvious, but it is not something you expect and so many people did not look down when they should have. One of them was my sister, Pauline. She entered the house and immediately fell into the pond. Bob's father looked at her and said, "I don't know why he keeps that durn thing there. Everybody's always walkin' into it."

Away from "The Brady Bunch," Bob's roles have been unusual and controversial. He starred in a 2-part "Medical Center — The Third Sex," in which he played a husband and father who underwent a trans-sexual operation. He was also in the NBC-TV movie, "The Secret Night Caller," where he was cast as a businessman by day and an obscene phone caller by night. He has also played in everything from Shakespeare to the Broadway comedy "Barefoot In The Park." He has also appeared as co-star on "The Defenders" as well as playing in shows such as "Mannix," "Father Knows Best," "Nurse," and others.

Robert Reed is extremely knowledgeable in many areas — art, music, fashion, so many things. Yet at heart he is a country boy from Oklahoma who is probably most comfortable wearing jeans, an old shirt, and driving with the windows rolled down on his Jaguar, listening to country music.

When Bob was on my show, I sang the song, "Memories." I looked over at him as I sang and noticed that tears were rolling down his face. Later he said to me, "You know, I didn't know it at the time, but those years on 'The Brady Bunch' were some of the happies years of my life."

FOOD FACTS

Did you know that the word, "salad," is derived from "salt," the sole ingredient originally used to season all salads?

•

Who eats ice cream at home? Adults over age 55 eat it an average of 56 times a year, far more than children.

•

Known as a fruit today, in 1893, the supreme court ruled it a vegetable . . . the tomato.

Beef & Biscuit Casserole

As Prepared by Robert Reed

Ingredients:

3 Tbsp. Dried Minced Onion
1-1¼ Lbs. Ground Beef
½ Cup Chopped Onion
¼ Cup Diced Green Chiles
1 8-Oz. Can Tomato Sauce
2 Tsp. Chili Powder
¾ Tsp. Garlic Salt
1 8-Oz. Can Refrigerated
    Buttermilk Biscuits
1½ Cups Shredded Monterey
    Jack and Cheddar Cheese
½ Cup Sour Cream
1 Egg Slightly Beaten

Directions:

Preheat oven to 375° F. Brown ground beef, chopped onion, and diced green chiles in pan, drain grease. Stir in tomato sauce, chili powder, garlic salt, and minced onion, simmer.

Separate refrigerated buttermilk biscuits into 10 biscuits, then separate again into 20 biscuits. Place 10 of the half-biscuits into bottom of 8 or 9-inch square glass baking dish.

Combine ½ cup shredded monterey jack and cheddar cheese with sour cream and egg, mix well. Remove meat from heat, stir in sour cream mixture. Place other 10 biscuits on top of meat mixture. Sprinkle remaining 1 cup of cheeses on top of dough. Bake at 375° F. for 30 minutes until golden brown.

4 servings

Notes

Mel Tillis

'vе always delighted in working with Mel Tillis. He's a genuinely warm, wonderful individual. I remember when I did a two-hour "Love Boat" with him, the entire cast and crew just loved him; he has that effect on you.

Mel has what he calls his "inconvenience," a stutter that makes speech more difficult for him, but it has not prevented him from becoming a success as an entertainer. As he explained to me, "Everybody has to have a dream if you expect to become successful. You have to dream and you have to live that dream if it's at all possible."

I think that philosophy is one reason Mel and I get along so well. I have also believed in dreams since the time I was a small child; and as an adult, I have found that many of them have come true. In fact, Mel's comments and his life remind me of the message on a greeting card I gave to a close friend of mine, a young woman who was dying of cancer. The card expressed my belief when it said, "Dreams bring joy to our lives. Believing brings life to our dreams."

Mel knew he wanted to be an entertainer from the time he was young. He told me that he used to build little play houses as a child, setting up a little stage and putting on shows with stick dolls and puppets. He would create his own shows, perform all the parts, and invite his neighbors to be his audience. The way he tells it, he was an instant success, especially with an elderly neighbor lady named Mrs. Smith, who regularly gave him standing ovations.

The experience of putting on shows for his neighbors was a good one for the young boy. Mel said that, at a small

age, he realized that no one was immune to laughter. He explained, "The sooner I realized that, the better off I was."

I too, believe that laughter is universal. I would almost rather make people laugh than do anything else.

Mel's first big break as an entertainer came when he moved to Nashville in the mid-1950's, obtaining a position as a guitar player in Minnie Pearl's band. It was a band that nurtured some of the best in country music, including Roger Miller who was then working as a fiddle player. The fiddle was not to be Roger's key to success, though. Mel laughingly called him the "worst fiddle player you ever heard in your life."

Mel brought a major change to country music by emphasizing the characters and situations in what amounted to stories told through song. He became famous for such records as "Detroit City," "Ruby, Don't Take Your Love To Town," and "Mental Revenge." He has won numerous country music awards and has appeared on talk shows ranging from the "Tonight Show" to "Late Night With David Letterman," the latter a program from which I seem to have been banned.

When I was on the Tonight Show with David Letterman hosting, I made the mistake of answering quite honestly about the poverty I experienced as a child. I told him that we were so poor I had to walk 3 miles to school in the snow. Half the time our shoes had big holes in them, pieces of cardboard stuffed inside to try and protect our feet. I never had a new pair of shoes. I usually wore hand-me-downs that were already worn out.

I had always loved to read and one year my family couldn't afford my school books. That year, for Christmas, my older sister, Pauline, gave me my reader and that really was such a joy for me.

David, whose buck teeth have become almost a trademark, said, "Wow, you really *were* poor. I guess I wasn't that poor. We didn't have those problems. We always had

the things that we needed and I guess, compared to you, we were wealthy."

I couldn't resist saying, "Obviously your folks weren't too wealthy or they would have had your teeth fixed." The audience roared with laughter but David never had me on his show. I was only kidding, David!

Mel Tillis explained that his family worked in the fields in Florida when he was a little boy. He said, "Times were hard; it was the Depression. We worked on the strawberry fields and on the truck farms. We would come in for lunch and Mama would have prepared this Country Summer Day Dinner for us. She would have it all fixed and ready to go on the stove."

Country Summer Day Dinner

As Prepared by Mel Tillis

Ingredients:

CHOPS AND GREENS

6 Pork Chops, Center Cut
Greens From 6 Turnips,
　Cleaned
6 Med. Turnips, Washed, Peeled,
　Sliced ¼" Thick
1 Tsp. Sugar
Grease from 10 Pc. White Bacon,
　Fried (Salt Pork)
2 Cups Water

POTATO SALAD

6 Med. Potatoes, Peeled,
　Washed, Diced
5 Eggs
2 Med. Onions, Diced
½ Bell Pepper, Diced
6 Lg. Sweet Pickles, Diced
1 Small Jar Pimientos
1 Stalk Celery, Diced
4 Tbsp. Salad Dressing (Not
　Mayonnaise)
3 Tbsp. Mustard

Directions:

Place turnip greens in large pot, sprinkle sugar on greens. Lay turnip slices on top of greens, lay pork chops on greens and turnips. Pour grease from fried white bacon over greens, chops, and turnips. Add water to pot, cook on high until water starts to boil. Reduce to low heat, cook covered about 45-60 minutes until greens are done.

Bring diced potatoes and eggs to boil, reduce heat and simmer until potatoes are soft (approx. 10 minutes). Mix onions, bell pepper, pickles, pimientos, celery, salad dressing, and mustard together. Peel eggs and slice, add eggs and potatoes to mixture. Refrigerate until meal is ready.

(Serve both with fresh green onions, sliced beets, cornbread, and blackberry cobbler).

6 servings

Notes

Harry Blackstone, Jr.

arry Blackstone, Jr. was one of the most suave, articulate, and handsome men on my show, when I could find him. You see, Harry is an illusionist, a magician, a man who is one of the most successful entertainers in his field in the world. He was named America's Bicentennial Magician in 1976. He was one of two Americans invited to perform for Queen Elizabeth II during her Silver Jubilee Gala at Windsor Castle. He was also awarded the Star of Magic, an honor received by only 11 individuals in 80 years.

Despite his success, Harry Blackstone, Jr., tried to avoid the field of magic. He is the son of The Great Blackstone, a pioneer illusionist who developed some of the world's most successful magic acts in history. At six months of age, his father began using him for some of his illusions. Then, at 4, he began learning mental telepathy tricks. By 7 he was traveling with his father, gradually learning the craft, including such tricks as the dancing handkerchief, the vanishing bird cage, and the buzz-saw.

Harry was torn among several careers at first. He was a cowboy at one time, a linguist, an actor and an expert in theater production and management. He felt that if he went into a career as a magician, the public would feel that he was not as good as his father. He wanted to be respected in his own right, not as a "kid" who was imitating what his father did so well. "Quite frankly, I believed that one magician in the family was plenty and that if I, too, worked as a magician people would say, 'Oh, he's O.K., but did you ever see his father do that illusion?' I thought it best to try another field."

Harry graduated from the University of Texas, joined the Army, and was assigned to Japan because he was fluent in

Oriental languages. While there, he became the first Occidental to appear in an otherwise all Japanese production of "The Teahouse Of The August Moon." Then he obtained a part-time job at an Austin, Texas TV station owned by then Senator Lyndon B. Johnson and his wife, Lady Bird. They needed a magician for a commercial that was being filmed so he used his years of training to handle the job himself. It was so successful that he began performing on a children's show and appearing at parties, including one on the LBJ ranch. He finally admitted that he loved magic and that he might as well make a career of it.

While working on his act, Harry took another detour. He worked as a producer with the Smothers Brothers' variety show on CBS Television. He also produced their Las Vegas act and managed three west coast companies of the Broadway musical, "Hair."

The Great Blackstone died in 1965 and his friends encouraged Harry, Jr., to work full time in the field. "I heard and understood them, but for many reasons, I resisted. Finally, one day, a light went on in the back of my head. It said: 'Do it!' I resolved then and there to do everything within my power to continue and enhance the name of Blackstone and all it stands for in the worlds of magic and entertainment."

The results of that decision have been spectacular. Harry has played to record crowds in clubs, on tour, and on Broadway. In fact, when he opened BLACKSTONE! at the Majestic Theatre in New York on May 19, 1980, the show ran for 112 performances. It was the longest running illusion show in the history of New York theater.

As Harry explained, "The response was most gratifying. I was particularly pleased that the audience and reviewers accepted me on my own terms. My father will always be remembered and revered. It was not easy, in his shadow, to establish my own identity. But, I have done so and I'm very proud of it. He would be too."

One of Harry's personal interests has been the study of people who claim to be able to do such amazing things with their minds as bend spoons and move objects. He said that no matter how famous the individual, he has yet to find one example that could not be explained through a knowledge of sleight of hand and other common tricks. They are nothing but illusionists who deny the false reality of what they do. It is a comment I have heard from others whom I respect, even though I do believe in ESP and thought projection at times.

The recipe Harry prepared was delicious, but he again showed off his skill. I was standing next to him when he put a lid on his pot, then took it off and there was a small rabbit. You would think that being so close, seeing the utensils, and knowing what was possible, I would have seen some trick. But the reality is that, even though I was standing next to him when he produced that rabbit from what I thought was a container of hot food, I had and have no idea how he did it. He is an amazing man.

Steak

As Prepared by Harry Blackstone, Jr.

Ingredients:

4 Sirloin Steaks, 6 Oz. Each
7 Tbsp. Butter
4 Tbsp. Shallots, Chopped
2½ Cups Sliced Mushrooms,
   Fresh
2 Tbsp. Worcestershire Powder
1½ Tsp. Cumin
¼ Cup Brandy
Salt
Pepper
2 Tsp. Chopped Parsley

Directions:

In small skillet slightly brown 4 tbsp. butter, shallots, and mushrooms over low heat. Place 4 sirloin steaks between sheets of wax paper. Pound to 1/3 inch thick. Add Worcestershire powder to the skillet, add cumin, and heat to bubbling boil.

In separate chafing dish, add remaining 3 tbsp. butter and heat until butter browns and add steaks for 2 minutes on one side, then turn once and cook other side for additional 1-2 minutes. Add the original sauce from the small skillet, and add brandy; flame all. Transfer to serving dish, add salt and pepper to taste and parsley to decorate.

4 servings

Notes

Shelly West

helly West is the daughter of another guest, top country singer Dottie West, and the relationship between the two women is beautiful. So often in this business, there is competition or hard feelings between parent and child. But Dottie adores her daughter, delights in her solo career, and enjoys working with Shelly whenever she can. In fact, although Shelly did not have her first solo release until 1983, as far back as 1975, Shelly was a back-up singer for her mother during a two year period of touring.

Shelly's voice is warm and rich, like a cello. She said that her mother has been like a teacher and she a pupil, Dottie willing to share all her knowledge.

Oddly, though Shelly wanted to be a singer since she was very young, she didn't have the courage to say so until she was around 17. However, she was determined to have a career despite being slightly intimidated by the success of her mother.

Shelly's first solo, "Jose Cuervo," climbed to number one of the country charts. It then became Billboard Magazine's #1 charted country single for 1983. This was followed by such successes as "Flight 309 To Tennessee" and "Another Motel Memory." Later she teamed with David Frizzell to produce such major hits as "You're The Reason God Made Oklahoma," "Texas State Of Mind," "Husbands And Wives," "I Just Came Here To Dance," and "Silent Partners." Shelly works both with David and alone today, explaining, "The duet will always be special to me, and we plan to work together as much as we can in the future. But David and I are also grateful to our fans for the success of our solo careers."

During the cooking segment of my show, Shelly and I were joking and began throwing food at each other. We both became a little embarrassed, afraid that we might influence children the wrong way. Yet I remember as kids having food fights, much to my mother's dismay, even though I suspect that all kids do that at one time or another.

There was an instance when I was making a Wesson Oil commercial and slipped with some of the food. I swore, saying, "Oh, Shit!" There was a child on the set and I immediately put my hands over his ears, saying, "You didn't hear that. I can just hear you now, 'Na-Na-Na-Na-Na-a. Mrs. Brady swears. Mrs. Brady swears.' " Fortunately the commercial was being taped and we were able to reshoot the scene. However, you can still see the part that was taken out on Dick Clark's bloopers show.

I asked Shelly what her biggest dream is and she said to sing in a filled auditorium holding 100,000 people. I think that I share that dream, though I would like to have that achievement when I am 95. Now, is that too much to ask?

More seriously, Shelly said, "What I enjoy most is singing songs that move people. If the song is sad, I hope they will feel that; if it's happy, I want them to feel good. And when I go on stage, I put all my own troubles aside and sing for the people. I love it."

Now Shelly is expanding into television and movies. She has been seen on the "Tonight Show," "Solid Gold," "Merv Griffin," and others. She had a cameo role in the Clint Eastwood film "Honky Tonk Man" and she is looking to expand her work in this area. She is a remarkable talent, and it appears that she will be as successful in her own right as her mother, Dottie West, has been.

FOOD FACTS

There are seven thousand varieties of rice in the world.

●

Parsley contains three times as much vitamin C as an orange and twice as much iron as spinach.

●

The average American eats about one-half ton of cheese in a lifetime.

●

Sauerkraut did not originate in Germany — but in China, thousands of years ago.

●

Butter was originally used in Europe and the Mideast as — a skin moisturizer.

●

The onion is a member of the lily family.

Wiener Schnitzel

As Prepared by Shelly West

Ingredients:

1 Lb. Veal (Thin Sliced)
1 Cup All-Purpose Flour
  (Seasoned with Salt & Papper
  to Taste)
1 Cup Bread Crumbs
6 Eggs, Well Beaten
½ Cup Fresh Chopped Parsley
2 Lemons (Thin Sliced)
2 Tbsp. Wesson Oil
2 Med. Yellow Squash
2 Med. Zucchini
2 Med. Carrots

Directions:

Pound veal very thin, coat with flour. Dip into eggs, dip in bread crumbs. Fry veal over medium heat in oil. Sprinkle parsley and add lemon slices while frying. When meat is brown on one side, turn over, brown on other side. When meat is done, transfer to warm serving dish.

Sliver yellow squash, zucchini, and carrots with a vegetable peeler. Saute vegetables lightly. Serve with veal.

3 servings

Notes

The Whites

I find The Whites to be a very special family. The mainstays of the group are Buck White and his daughters, Sharon and Cheryl. All three sing in addition to playing, and a younger child, Rosie, plays percussion with the back-up group of musicians they use.

The Whites are an unusual family, fun loving, and a delight to know, yet have very conservative religious and personal values. In fact, Buck White deliberately abandoned a full-time musical career in order to assure his family the upbringing he wanted them to have.

Buck's early musical career involved his working as a part-time honkytonk piano player and singer. While still in high school in Wichita Falls, Texas, he and some friends put together a band that played in Vernon, Texas, 50 miles away. Most of his work was on the mandolin and piano where he developed great skill.

Buck's wife, Pat, was a singer, but the two of them met when she was attending a show where her brother was playing. Later Buck, Pat, and two friends formed The Down Home Folks, a group that played primarily on weekends. Eventually Cheryl and Sharon took the places of the other couple, though that would not occur until 1967.

There were a number of Nashville musicians who respected Buck White's work so much that they wanted him to play with them, but Buck was a realist about the music business. Until you are an established star, the music business is an uncertain way to earn a living. Trying to raise a family without knowing how steady the work is going to be is unsettling. Since Buck was a skilled pipe fitter, he moved his family to Arkansas and worked in the building trades, playing music only on weekends.

Cheryl talks about that time with pride. She remembers Buck coming home during the winter with his hands frozen from handling pipe all day. He would have to soak them right away, then work his fingers by playing the mandolin after dinner. There were times when he had difficulty working the strings and they feared that the work might eventually hurt his ability to play. Fortunately, that was not the case and his music is better than ever.

By 1971, the White family had moved to Nashville where they began touring on the bluegrass festival circuit. Two years later, Pat retired and Buck began sharing vocals with his two daughters. The group called The Whites, as we know them today, was formed.

The story of The Whites is not uncommon. The music business is a vocation that can be quite difficult. I have always felt that I had two vocations in life, being a mother and making music. I believe that God gives us certain talents in life and that it is up to us to use them. When I realized early on that I had the ability to make people feel good, to entertain them, to lift their spirits a little bit, I took that knowledge very seriously. That is why I work so hard at what I do, as do people like The Whites.

Sharon and Cheryl White were both skilled in the kitchen. They explained that when they were growing up, they each had certain chores related to getting the dinner ready.

I too had the same experience growing up. Both my parents worked and it was necessary for the 10 of us kids to fill in and do whatever had to be done to get all the work completed.

I think that country kids learn to fend for themselves at an early age. I remember learning how to cook, then joining the 4-H Club and baking a devil's food cake that won me a trip to the state fair in Indianapolis. I got to enjoy all the rides, the animals, and all the wonderful sights. It was a very special event.

Sharon White is now married to Ricky Skaggs and they have an adorable little girl, Molly Kate. Ricky recently pro-duced some of their albums and the family is extremely close.

I know that Buck is very proud of his family. He explained that when you have a dream, as he did for his children, you can make it happen.

The Whites and I share that belief in dreams, though all of us recognize that when your dreams come true, you have a responsibility to others. For example,I hate to see a performer go on stage and not obviously have a good time. We all work so hard to entertain, it is important to share that joy with the audience. When you do, and I know The Whites succeed in this, everyone is happy, their spirits lifted, their troubles either forgotten or, for the moment, no longer so overwhelming.

Chicken Enchiladas

As Prepared by Sharon, Cheryl & Buck White

Ingredients:

*4 Lg. Chicken Breasts,
   Cooked, Boned, and Diced
3 Cups Monterey Jack Cheese,
   Grated (with Jalapenos)
1 Lg. Onion, Diced
1 4-Oz. Can Diced Green Chiles
1 Cup Sour Cream
3 Tbsp. Butter
2 10½-Oz. Cans Cream of
   Mushroom Soup
1 Jar Picante Sauce (Med. Hot)
10 Flour Tortillas,
   Oven Warmed
Sour Cream
   (to Taste, Garnish)
Avocados, Sliced (Garnish)*

Directions:

Combine in large mixing bowl: chicken breasts, (cooked, boned, and diced) grated monterey jack cheese (with jalapenos if desired), diced onion, diced green chiles and sour cream. Add ½ can cream of mushroom soup, mix.

Melt 1 tbsp. butter in bottom of 13x9x2" glass baking dish. Fill 10 warm tortillas with chicken mix. Sprinkle 1 tbsp. picante sauce on each, roll up. Place seam side down into baking dish.

Melt 2 tbsp. butter in saucepan, add remaining soup mix. Pour over enchiladas. Bake uncovered 30 minutes at 350° F. until brown. Garnish with sour cream to taste and avocado slices.

Serve with rice and refried beans, and salad (chopped lettuce, apple, and salad dressing)

4 servings

Notes

Joe Bonsall

Joe Bonsall, the tenor with the Oak Ridge Boys, began singing because he thought it was an easier way to make a living than getting beat up. While so many of my guests have had their roots in the country, Joe's background was as urban as you can get. He was raised in Philadelphia, a skinny kid who ran with a group of young toughs in what was called the K&A Gang. Unfortunately, he had more spirit than fighting ability and regularly ended up on the losing end of violence. He also recognized that his friends had serious problems, five of them eventually committing suicide.

Despite the type of running around he was doing, Joe was liked by some of the nicer boys in the neighborhood and they tried to interest him in the contemporary Christian quartets who regularly sang in the area. "I thought going to one of those concerts was a pansy thing to do," he explained to me. However, when he kept getting hurt and bloodied, he finally agreed to attend a concert by the Blackwood Brothers and the Eastman Quartet. He was hooked immediately.

The message of the gospel songs was important to Joe, but what really interested him was singing in general. He realized that it was an area where he could excel regardless of his physical size or abilities. He was neither big enough nor good enough to join high school athletic teams, but he could join the choir.

Joe's first professional group was the Faith Four Gospel Quartet which he helped form. They journeyed from church to church, performing for handouts and selling custom made albums after the services. Unfortunately, they earned only enough to pay for the Dodge Van they purchased for travel and the cost of cutting the records. Still, as all entertainers are unhappily aware, there are times when breaking even can be considered a success.

Eventually Joe met another young singer named Richard Sterban who sold clothing in a Gimbels Department Store in Philadelphia and was singing bass with a group called the Keystone Quartet. When he wasn't working at his sales job with a sugar refinery, he followed Richard around at the store, talking music.

The Keystone Quartet went through a transformation and needed another voice. Joe was hired for a promised salary of $75 per week, barely enough to make ends meet in the early 1960's. Unfortunately the group had more hope than they had paying customers. Joe was lucky if he made $75 in a month with the group.

Desperate for greater success so they could stop working supplementary jobs, the Keystone Quartet moved to Buffalo, New York, where they sang as well as acted as booking agents for other gospel groups, including the Oak Ridge Boys. "The Oaks were the innovative quartet in gospel music. They performed gospel with a rock approach, had a band, wore bell bottom pants and grew their hair long," Joe told me.

The rest of the story became music history. Richard Sterban joined the Oak Ridge Boys in 1972, Joe following a year later when an opening for a tenor occurred. The remaining members of the Keystones had other areas of interest so the group would have disbanded regardless.

As I have stressed many times, entertaining is a giving profession. It is one where your job is to give the audience a few hours of total enjoyment. You want them to like you, but you want them to enjoy themselves and have fun. The success of the Oak Ridge Boys reflects their dedication to that end. For example, Joe commented:

"At this point, a lot of physical things have changed. We have others doing things for us. We all remember the days when we drove our own buses, carried in our own sound system, put up the lights, tore down the equipment when we were through—we did everything. Although we have folks doing all of those things now we have GOT to be great. We've got to be the best we can possibly be every time we go on stage. There's a mental pressure every night, but a pressure I enjoy."

The other interesting aspect of Joe and the other Oak Ridge Boys is their involvement with the National Committee for the Prevention of Child Abuse (NCPCA). The committee is all volunteer and located throughout the United States. Their aim is to understand the stress factors that can cause child abuse, then reach parents who are at risk so they can stop the abuse before it starts. The Oaks have made endorsements, arranged concerts and benefits, and handled other tasks, something unusual for them since they normally avoid commercial endorsements, not wishing to become a part of product marketing. However, this is one area close to their hearts. As Joe has explained many times, children have a right to be children.

"We must handle adult problems and adult situations as adults. I think it's a very sad thing when adults who can't handle their problems take them out on their children. I don't care if those problems are pressure, business, sexual, whatever. It's unfortunate to make children the ones to suffer for problems that we as adults cannot handle."

Italian Eggplant Casserole

As Prepared by Joe Bonsall

Ingredients:

1 Large Eggplant
2 Eggs
⅓ Cup Flour
⅓ Cup Italian Bread Crumbs
¼ Cup Wesson Oil
1 32-Oz. Jar Spaghetti Sauce
6 Oz. Mozzarella Cheese,
   Grated
⅓ Cup Parmesan Cheese,
   Grated
1 Tbsp. Dried Minced Onions
Lg. Frying Pan
2 Qt. Casserole Dish
Red Chili Powder (to Taste)

Directions:

Peel and slice eggplant into ½ inch slices. Beat 2 eggs. Mix flour and Italian bread crumbs in baggie. Heat oil in frying pan on medium heat. Prehcat oven to 400°.

Dip eggplant into egg and shake in baggie. Brown slices in frying pan about 3 to 4 minutes per side (3 at a time). Lay on paper towel, continue until all are fried.

Layer casserole dish with: half of eggplant slices, half of parmesan cheese, 10 oz. of spaghetti sauce, red chili powder and 3 oz. of mozzarella cheese. Sprinkle dried minced onions on top. Layer rest of ingredients. Cook uncovered 20 to 30 minutes. Serve with tossed salad and garlic bread.

4-6 servings

Notes

Della Reese

ella Reese is one of the most remarkable entertainers in show business. She is a singer and songwriter whose hits range from Gospel to pop to her biggest hit, "Don't You Know," which is actually from the Puccini opera, "La Boheme." She is an actress who has done both comedy and drama. And she is an entertainer who not only was a regular guest on such classics as "The Ed Sullivan Show" and "The Perry Como Show," but found time to be a guest host on the "Tonight Show." Also, Della was the first black woman to have her own television show. In 1969 and 1970, the program "Della" was syndicated by RKO/General.

But aside from her professional accomplishments, one of the things I like best about Della is her incredible energy and a "real spirit" that just emanates from her. When I hugged her on my show, I literally could feel that power within her.

I suspect some of Della's intense spirituality comes from her having survived two close calls with death. One time she collapsed on the Johnny Carson Show and had to have emergency surgery to save her life. Another time she fell through a plate glass door and was saved by her daughter. But instead of becoming depressed by her misfortune, Della became closer to God, today holding regular church services in her home.

Most recently, Della formed a professional Gospel music group called "Brilliance." She chose members who are from radically different backgrounds and have unique styles

that can blend together like "facets of a diamond," as she explains.

"Brilliance" includes O.C. Smith who has a background primarily in country and folk music; Eric Storm made his reputation in musical comedy and light opera; Vermettya Royster began with the original Clara Ward Singers and, later, was one of Ray Charles Raylettes. In addition, there is

Merry Clayton who sang with singers Bobby Darin and Mick Jagger. It is part of Della's musical genius that she can take such seemingly disparate voices and blend them into a group that lives up to its name — "Brilliance."

One of Della's philosophies for success in life is to work on your problems from the inside out. First you must change what is in your heart and then your appearance, your life, and your world begins to fall into place. It is a philosophy I have always shared.

For example, people often tell me how good I look. I feel that this is because I believe that if my thoughts are right and my philosophy of life is intact, it will show externally. It is important to concentrate on what you are thinking about, what you are doing to take charge of your life, to be responsible for your own actions. As Della and I both agree, when you work from the inside out, the results are bound to show.

Della was raised in an apartment that had a skylight. Like so many of us, she began singing when she was young. Della discovered that her voice bounced off the roof, enabling her to hear herself and helping her to improve. This type of situation is one every singer tries to find so that they can hear themselves before performing. In fact, when I'm on the road, I'm delighted when my dressing room has a shower. Just before going on stage I'll step into the shower stall, leaving the water off, of course, and vocalize a bit. There is incredible resonance as the sound bounces off the concrete or tile walls and it helps me make certain that my voice is warmed up and ready to go.

Della claims the chicken dish she prepared came about by accident. She had been performing, came home, and discovered that there was very little food in the house. If she was going to eat, she would have to improvise with such seemingly unrelated items as oranges, chicken, peanut butter, and ginger. Fortunately this is a woman who improvises as brilliantly in the kitchen as she does with her singing. Once you blend the ingredients the way Della describes, you will have a surprisingly delicious taste sensation.

Broccoli Chicken Thighs

As Prepared by Della Reese

Ingredients:

8 Chicken Thighs, Boned or Not
  Boned
2 Cups Butter
¼ Cup Cooking Wine
1 Tbsp. Peanut Butter
1¼ Cups Orange Juice
1 Tbsp. Orange Peel, Grated
2 Tsp. Salt
¼ Tsp. Ginger
2/3 Cup Brown Sugar
1 Cup Sour Cream
2 Pkg. Frozen Chopped Broccoli,
Cooked and Drained
2 Tomatoes, Cut into Wedges

Directions:

Preheat oven to 375°. Simmer chicken thighs in butter in large frying pan 10-12 minutes until somewhat browned. Add cooking wine, keep cooking, about 5 minutes more. Remove chicken to baking pan skin side up, in single layer (don't stack).

Mix together: peanut butter, orange juice, grated orange peel, salt, ginger, brown sugar, and sour cream.* Reserve ¼ cup of mixture, pour rest over chicken in pan. Cook uncovered until done (fork tender.)

Remove from oven, arrange 2 pkgs. cooked chopped broccoli and tomatoes cut into wedges attractively around chicken.

*Pour reserved sauce over broccoli, return to oven for 5 minutes.

*You may add other vegetables to taste, such as tiny ears of corn, etc.

4-6 servings

Notes

T. Graham Brown

T. Graham Brown is typical of so many of the newly "discovered" singers in show business; he is an "overnight sensation" with 13 years in the business. He also has a reputation as a man who likes to "shake things up" when he makes an appearance, though the reality when he was my guest was slightly different — not that he didn't reveal some of his eccentricities on my show, of course. He wore a shirt covered with dinosaurs and his trademark prescription sun glasses. But the reality is that his outrageous behavior is often a cover for a very nice, rather shy young man.

I'd say that T. Graham Brown fits the myth of the overnight sensation because he started his career as Tony Brown working his way through college with a partner named Dirk Howell. Tony, or T. Graham as he is known today, was raised in the tiny community of Arabi, Georgia, which "had a population of 300, including pine trees, sand, and rattlesnakes," as he explains it. He attended the University of Georgia and began singing for such groups as Reo Diamond and The Rack Of Spam. While neither of those groups became household words, a singing act with a friend, Dirk Howell, became extremely popular both with fraternity parties and at the Athens Holiday Inn. The Holiday Inn appearances were so popular during their college years that the motel canceled plans to build a convention center and, instead, built a lounge four times the size of the original. It was already obvious that Tony had the ability to draw a crowd.

T. Graham met his wife, Sheila, while at the University of Georgia. It was a lucky meeting for him because she believed in his abilities enough to move with him to Nashville where she worked two jobs so they could pay their bills. During that time he was working wherever he could, writing jingles and making demonstration tapes. Their first year in Nashville he earned less than $900. However, he likes to say that persistence is what helped him survive until he became successful. He said, "There have been so many times when I've been just dead broke, when I wanted to quit and get a regular job and forget about it 'cause it gets pretty discouraging sometimes. But if you quit, it ain't never gonna happen."

That term, "persistence," is very important. Most everyone who has made it in this business has paid a lot of dues. Talent alone won't do it. Not even hard work, alone, will do it. But persistence *will* do it. You've just got to hang in there a little longer than the other person.

This idea certainly has been a part of my philosophy. When I rehearse I am usually the first one there and the last one to leave. I don't know any other way to make the work good. And maybe that's part of success, that your work is never quite good enough in your own opinion, so you are always working to improve.

Young people will often come to me and ask me what I think is important and I will tell them to retain their individuality. They should find out who they are and build on that. They should not be a poor imitation of someone else. They should be themselves, building on their roots and going on from there. No one ever makes it by pretending to be someone else.

T. Graham wore sun glasses on the show, a trademark of many young performers. His were different in that they were prescription sun glasses to help him see better under the hot lights. Unfortunately many entertainers seem to use sun glasses to hide from their audience as I once hid from mine as a small child. It was only when I grew up that I realized how important it is to make eye contact with your audience.

Now I want to know how my audience is reacting. Are they enjoying the performance? I want to see their laughter and their tears. I want to be certain I am touching their hearts and their lives, to move someone in the audience.

T. Graham Brown is at that point in his career where anything is possible. He is working regularly, including writing several successful jingles along with his extremely successful records such as "I Tell It Like It Used To Be," his first LP on which he had several major singles. He also tries to find time to engage in what he considers his favorite pasttime, watching the "Andy Griffith Show." However, he claims true success will come when he achieves the following:

"I want to be a great human being, a wonderful cat, have three Number One singles, have my own Saturday morning cartoon show, and triple my watchings of the Andy Griffith Show!"

Cheesy "Spam" Bake

As Prepared by T. Graham Brown

Ingredients:

6-8 Potatoes, Sliced
3 Tbsp. Butter
1 Small Onion, Chopped
½ Tsp. Paprika
⅛ Tsp. Dried Thyme
2 Tbsp. Flour
1 Tsp. Dried Mustard
1 Tsp. Salt
⅛ Tsp. Pepper
1 Cup Light Cream
2 Cups "Spam" Cubed
1 Cup Sharp Cheddar Cheese,
  Shredded

Directions:

Preheat oven to 350° F. Cook sliced potatoes in boiling salted water 15 minutes. Drain potatoes, saving 1 cup of cooking liquid. Place potatoes in casserole dish.

Melt butter in large skillet. Add chopped onion and brown slightly. Add paprika, thyme, flour, dried mustard, salt and pepper. Stir in reserved liquid and light cream, cook until thick, stirring constantly. Add cubed Spam and ½ cup shredded sharp cheddar cheese.

Pour sauce over potatoes, toss lightly. Top with ½ cup shredded sharp cheddar cheese and bake at 350° F for 45 minutes. Serve with green salad.

6-8 servings

Notes

Freddy Fender

reddy Fender has been entertaining audiences for 30 years. Our personal friendship goes back a long time as well. We have appeared together on the "Tonight Show" and "Hollywood Squares," and as a result of one of those shows, I was delighted to learn that Freddy was recently elected to the Hispanic Hall Of Fame.

Freddy's background initially created some problems in gaining a national audience. His earliest records, in the 1950's, were all in Spanish and meant only for that audience. They were well received, but his audience was too small to bring him to the attention of many of the potential record buyers.

Next, Freddy combined American country music with the beauty and sadness of Mexican ballads. That led to the style that is often called "Tex-Mex Rockabilly." However, by 1969, having both soloed and played with numerous other musicians, he returned to the San Benito Valley where he was raised, abandoning most of his music in order to work as a mechanic. He continued to play on weekends but did not see music as ever again being part of a career.

Freddy had other goals during this period as well. He returned to high school and earned his diploma, then went on to college, thinking about getting a degree in sociology so he could work in prison reform. However, everything changed in 1975 when he recorded "Before The Next Teardrop Falls" and "Wasted Days And Wasted Nights," both of which won gold records. His album went gold that

year and he won all manner of awards, including "Best Male Artist of 1975." Freddy was back in music full time, his career continuing to thrive.

Yet with all his success, Freddy has a nervousness about performing that we all share. I know for myself, my shyness goes back to when I was 2 years old and would perform for the family. We were extremely poor, so at the end of my songs my mother had me pass the hat, aunts, uncles, and others putting change in it. That action so embarrassed me that I would either have all the guests close their eyes while I sang or they would keep them open and I would close mine.

When he was on the show, Freddy prepared a Mexican dish using two of my favorite foods — tortilla chips and refried pinto beans. Growing up poor, pinto beans and Irish potatoes were staples in our household because they are both nutritious and filling. The only problem is that pinto beans give you gas. As I explained on the "Tonight Show," I always had so much gas that my feet never touched the ground until I arrived in New York and discovered what was happening.

Despite our joking about the food, Freddy has always stressed that young people should not be ashamed of their heritage. The recipe Freddy made is one common among people who have lived in poverty. It is high in nutritional value yet inexpensive. And his attitude is that there is dignity and worth in everyone. A lack of money does not make someone a failure.

FOOD FACTS

Mediterranean street vendors were selling short-order fried fish, cucumbers, onions — and freshly grilled meats — as early as 2000 B.C.

•

The richest known source of vitamins, minerals, and amino acids which also contains protein and natural antibiotics and is considered a complete food is — bee pollen.

•

The residents of New Orleans use more ketchup per person than any other city in the United States. But Salt Lake City residents eat the most marshmallows and candy bars, while Dallas is the popcorn consumer capital.

Migas Rancheras

As Prepared by Freddy Fender

Ingredients:

1 Dozen Corn Tortillas
Wesson Oil
4 Canned Tomatoes, Chopped
2-3 Eggs
½ Onion, Chopped
2-3 Peppers (Jalapeno or Chili),
* Diced*
30 Oz. Refried Beans
8 Oz. Chorizo, Chopped
* (Mexican Sausage)*

Directions:

Tear or cut corn tortillas into 1-inch pieces. Cover bottom of skillet with oil. Fry tortillas in oil over high heat. Add tomatoes to skillet. Stir in chopped onion and 2-3 jalapeno or chili peppers, diced. Simmer until tender.

Brown chorizo on high in second skillet. Add refried beans to chorizo (once sausage has broken up), stir until hot.

Stir 2-3 eggs into tomato mixture. Cook until eggs are done.

4 servings

Notes

David Frizzell

I thoroughly enjoyed David Frizzell, a man with one of those handsome, craggy faces. He calls himself a "honky-tonk singer," a term I have heard used with other musicians as well. Generally this means a singer who has really paid his dues, singing in a lot of bars where people are smoking and drinking, singing throughout the night while people cry in their beer and want to hear a rather mournful type of song. Now, that builds stamina.

People don't realize how rough it is along the way for singers in clubs. You start out anywhere you can get an engagement, knowing that for much of the audience, your singing is of less importance than elevator music. You sing to people who don't particularly want to hear you, as well as to those so drunk that, no matter how much they seem to enjoy you, they will probably forget your performance in the morning.

Yet, all along there are people who care, who listen and appreciate your efforts. Their interest keeps you going, keeps you trying to do your best. Their interest motivates you to constantly improve and hope you can move on to clubs where the singing is the reason they are there. It's an extremely hard life and many entertainers leave the business because they cannot take it. Being a honky-tonk singer thus says a lot about the courage, stamina, and determination of a man such as David.

I think that one of the things that I like about the kind of country music David sings is that it does tell the truth. It doesn't fool around. It tells of lost love, of tragedies, of happiness. Country music really tells a story and the honky-tonk singers — men such as David, George Jones, Merle Haggard, and the rest — lay their hearts on the line with their music.

During the show, David talked with his small son, Jonathan, who was in the audience. That touching action reminded me of just how tough our business can be on our private lives. David has this adorable child, yet when he has to go on the road, they have to be separated, sometimes for long periods of time. This is tough for anyone.

When my own children were small and I would go on the road, or even now, when my kids are grown but I have to be away from them, it pains me to be separated, I love them so much. And when they're small and they're changing so rapidly, you know you're missing the tooth coming in, or they're starting to crawl or walk, and you just don't want to miss a moment of that. It's one of the very difficult things about being a performer and having to be on the road. We can only pray that our children understand our crazy need to be in this business.

I always tell young people that if they don't really have the deep down desire, the *need* to be in the business, to be a singer, actor or performer, don't do it. If you just can't help it, that's the only reason to be in this business.

David has that drive, just as I do. He also has set standards for himself related to the type of music he sings, preferring country because it is what he loves. "I imagine a lot of the singers today are singing pop music to get in where the bigger money is," he explained. "I don't really care about that. I'd like to stay closer to pure country. I want to do what I do, and I hope there's a market for it."

FOOD FACTS

Almost half the world's total corn production is grown in — the United States.

•

Medicines distilled in the 1500's by monasteries, such as Benedictine and Chartreuse, evolved into today's sweet alcoholic drinks called — cordials.

•

The average American eats more bananas than any other fruit — about eighteen pounds per year.

•

You can't trust a food by its name. Bombay duck is fish, prairie oysters are eggs, and Alaskan strawberries are beans.

Enchiladas Verdes

As Prepared by David Frizzell

Ingredients:

2 Tbsp. Wesson Oil
12 6-inch Tortillas
2 Cups Shredded Monterey
  Jack Cheese (8 Oz.)
¾ Cup Chopped Onion
¼ Cup Butter or Margarine
¼ Cup All-Purpose Flour
2 Cups Chicken Broth
1 4-Oz. Can Pickled
  Jalapeno Peppers
  (Rinsed, Seeded, & Chopped)
1 Cup Dairy Sour Cream
1 Medium Tomato
  Finely Chopped
½ Cup Onion Finely Chopped
¼ Cup Tomato Juice
½ Tsp. Salt

Directions:

Heat oil in small skillet. Dip tortillas in oil for 10 seconds or until limber. Drain on paper towel. Place 2 tbsp. cheese and 1 tbsp. onion on each tortilla and roll up. Place tortilla seam side down in 12x7½x2 inch baking dish.

In medium saucepan melt butter and blend in flour. Add chicken broth all at once. Cook over medium heat, stirring constantly until thickened and bubbly. Reserve 1 tbsp. chopped peppers, stir sour cream and remaining peppers from can into sauce. Cook, low heat until heated through, don't boil. Pour sauce over tortillas in dish.

Bake at 425° for 20 minutes, sprinkle remaining cheese over tortillas, return to oven for 5 minutes, or until cheese melts. In bowl, combine tomato, chopped onion, tomato juice, salt, and reserved peppers. (Pass with enchiladas.) Serve with Spanish rice and salsa.

4-6 servings

Notes

Eddie Rabbitt

ddie Rabbitt is an extremely talented, high energy performer who gives so much to his audience that he becomes a hard act to follow. I remember when he was opening for Dolly Parton and his show was so good, even a star like Dolly had to work extremely hard to maintain the excitement.

Rabbitt is not a stage name. It is actually Gaelic in origin, the family coming from Galway County, Ireland, in 1924. The name Rabbitt translates from the Gaelic to mean "counselor to chiefs."

Eddie's ancestors may be Irish, but like a surprising number of country, pop, and rock stars, he comes from New Jersey. His first taste in country music came when he was in Scouting, going on an overnight hike. When the boys made camp, the Scoutmaster pulled out a guitar and began playing country songs. It was Eddie's first exposure to such music and he was hooked. Then his father gave him the money— $37.50—to buy a guitar and he was on his way.

Tony Schwickrath, the Scoutmaster, was Eddie's first teacher. However, after helping Eddie master just two chords, Tony moved out of town. From then on, Eddie was on his own.

Like Eddie, I had some outside influences for my music, though they were less personal than a Scoutmaster. I loved the big screen musicals, especially the ones starring Jane Powell. I used to learn every song she ever sang. In fact, I even auditioned once singing to the accompaniment of a Jane Powell record, though I did not win.

The movies would come periodically to my small town's theater and I would be entranced. I would watch Jane, Gene Kelly, Fred Astaire, Judy Garland, and all the other greats, singing and dancing every step of the way to my home. The movies made me know that there was something better out there than the grinding poverty at home. They inspired me to think that one day I could make it in show business.

While Eddie has always been fascinated by traditional country music, he is a musician who keeps aware of the changes in the field. He feels that just repeating the styles of the old standards is not that good for the business. "I think things have to move to stay alive," he told me. "Water that doesn't move is stagnant water. I'd like to see something more clever done with country music, rather than trying to reproduce it as it was 25 years ago."

Eddie mentioned the group Alabama as typical of country stars who seek modifications in the field. "When they do a song like 'Mountain Music,' it's the same old thing in a way, but it's got a new sound. It's a little heavier beat, a more clever arrangement than the simplistic way it would have been done 20 years ago."

There was a time when Eddie thought he should be somewhat progressive with his name, changing it to Eddie Martin. This did not last long, his real last name, Rabbitt, being so distinctive. In fact, he has taken to playing off his last name, working with a touring band called "Hare Trigger" and having a publishing company called "Briarpatch Music."

Entertainers are frequently asked to change their names. There was a period when I was in the touring company of the stage show "Oklahoma!" A movie was going to be made from it and I was asked to audition for the lead. I was told that, if I got it, the company would want to change my name. I told them I would not stand for it, that if I was going to be successful, I would be successful despite my name. Besides, an actor or actress likes to see their name on the marquee. Florence Henderson has 17 letters, takes up a lot of space, and gets attention.

Oddly, the one person in my family who wanted to change her name was my daughter, Barbara Bernstein. My husband and I were concerned, wondering what motivated her thinking. While I am Catholic, my husband was Jewish and we thought, perhaps, she had encountered anti-Semitism. Maybe there were children teasing her about being Bernstein. We became quite concerned, not certain how to ask her the reason. Finally we thought we would simplify things by asking her what name she wanted, figuring that might give us a clue to her feelings. And what name did she want? "Maria Bernstein."

We all had a good laugh about that, though Barbara eventually did have to change her name. She became quite a talented actress and a member of the guild. Under union rules, no two entertainers may have the same name. There was a Barbara Bernstein in the guild and there was also a Barbara Henderson, the two names she wanted. Finally she became Barbara Chase, a name used by no other member.

Eddie's career has been extremely successful, though his personal life has been marked with tragedy. His son, Timmy, was born with severe liver damage. Two years before he appeared on my show, the baby was scheduled for a liver-transplant operation, there being no other hope for the child. That operation, an extremely delicate one, yet one which has had success, was performed in the hospital at Vanderbilt. Tragically, the boy died during the surgery.

From the time Timmy was born until after his death, Eddie spent little time performing. He didn't know what time he would have with his son, who lingered in the hospital, and he wanted to be with his family. It was a personal tragedy that also showed he has his values in order. He and his wife also have had the courage to start again, having another child despite their great emotional sadness.

Beef Bombay

As Prepared by Eddie Rabbitt

Ingredients:

4 Tbsp. Wesson Oil
1 Cup Diced Onion
1 Lb. Beef Filet,
  Cut into ½ inch Strips
2 Tsp. Salt
1 Tbsp. Curry Powder
1 Cup Beer
¼ Cup Grated Coconut
¼ Cup Sliced Almonds
½ Cup Chopped Apples
½ Lb. Carrots, Peeled and Cut
  into 4 Pieces
4 Potatoes, Peeled and
  Quartered

Directions:

*Heat Dutch Oven or large cooking pot with lid, add oil. Brown diced onion, remove onion.

Brown filet in same pan. Add salt, curry powder, beer, grated coconut, sliced almonds, chopped apples, quartered carrots, and potatoes to pot. Return onions to pot. Cover, simmer 4 hours until meat is tender.

*You can use a crock pot.

4 servings

Notes

Barbara Eden

I became one of Barbara Eden's fans when I saw her in the hit T.V. series, "How To Marry A Millionaire." Her career has been one that is extremely broad since she is both a singer and an actress. Her television series "I Dream Of Jeannie" was on the air for five years, the same length of time as "The Brady Bunch," and it continues to be seen in syndication. She starred in a record breaking tour of "Woman Of The Year" in which she played the ambitious, independent broadcast journalist Tess Harding, a role first played by Lauren Bacall on Broadway. When she was in the NBC movie "Harper Valley PTA" in February of 1980, it was the only program to out rate the Olympic Games being shown on a rival network during the same time slot.

Barbara is an extraordinarily beautiful woman with an extremely stunning figure, but she sometimes is accused of being stuck-up. People will tell her that she walked past them as though she never saw them. What they don't realize is that their comment is true. Barbara is extremely near-sighted and, if she is not wearing her glasses or contacts, she really cannot see them.

I can understand that problem. I was born with a hereditary ear disease that made hearing extremely difficult. I was so near to being deaf that many times people would go by me and become angry because I never responded when they spoke. They had no idea that I could not hear. Fortunately I was able to have surgery that dramatically corrected the problem, but such handicaps can lead others to misunderstand your reactions.

When Barbara first went to Hollywood, she was 19 years old, had been raised in Tucson, studied music at the San Francisco Conservatory, and sang weekends with bands in order to pay her way through San Francisco City College. She was so clean cut and nice that an executive at Warner Brothers commented, "You're a nice kid from a nice family. Go home!" However, Barbara refused to take such advice, determined to succeed. She continued to knock on doors throughout the day, then worked in a bank at night.

Both Barbara and I had gone on Bob Hope's 75th anniversary tour to Australia, and we were surprised by his incredible energy. We realized that the entertainers with so much staying power, George Burns, Bob Hope, and the rest, all rose from the ranks of Vaudeville. With Vaudeville you were constantly on stage, sometimes doing 13 or 14 shows a day. They had to develop a very different kind of energy in order to keep functioning effectively. However I did see one of the tricks that Bob Hope used to keep himself rested. Whenever he wasn't needed on stage, he would find a quiet place in the auditorium and go over to be by himself and rest. I find that I do that myself to conserve energy since so much energy is needed when you perform.

That Australian tour was one of the highlights of my life. At one point we were in Perth which is apparently one of the furthest points on the earth from the United States. I found myself swimming in the Indian Ocean and it surprised me. Here I was, this little country girl from Indiana, actually reaching the other side of the world. I have been to Australia several times since and it is one of my favorite places.

Barbara and I talked about the "I Dream Of Jeannie" series which was one of the favorites of my youngest daughter, Lizzie. She was in love with the harem costume Barbara had to wear.

Barbara also starred in the series "Harper Valley PTA" which was produced by some of the same people who produced "The Brady Bunch." We both had the right people around us and it was a wonderful experience. It is a delight when people have good attitudes and when the other actors are better than you are, challenging you to bring out the best from within.

Today Barbara is appearing in everything from films to nightclubs. She is extremely talented and beautiful and was a delightful guest on my show.

Lamb Ka-Bob

As Prepared by Barbara Eden

Ingredients:

1½ Cups Wesson Oil
¾ Cup Soy Sauce
¼ Cup Worcestershire Sauce
2 Tbsp. Dry Mustard
2¼ Tsp. Salt
1 Tbsp. Coarse Freshly Ground
  Black Pepper
½ Cup Wine Vinegar
1½ Tsp. Dried Parsley Flakes
2 Crushed Garlic Cloves
⅓ Cup Fresh Lemon Juice
1½ Lbs. Leg of Lamb,
  Cubed in 1" Squares
2 Doz. Cherry Tomatoes
3 Med. Zucchini,
  Sliced into Thick Chunks
2 Doz. Fresh Large Mushrooms
6 Lg. Onions, Quartered
1 Pkg. Thin Semolina Noodles,
  4 Oz.
1 Pkg. Pine Nuts, 4 Oz.
1 Pkg. Rice, 8 Oz.

Directions:

Mix first ten ingredients with an egg beater. Add lamb cubes to mixture. Marinate in refrigerator overnight.

The next day, cut onions into quarters and zucchini into chunks. Using long skewers, put the vegetables and the lamb cubes onto the skewers, making sure the onion quarters are next to the meat, for instance: cherry tomato, mushroom, meat, onion, zucchini, then start over.

Broil over charcoal, turning continuously. Prepare rice and semolina noodles according to package. Brown pine nuts in oil or butter and mix all three together.

Serve lamb ka-bob over rice mixture.

4-6 servings

Notes

Jerry Clower

Jerry Clower is a man who likes to call himself the "mouth of the South of the Yazoo River." He is from Yazoo City, Mississippi. He says he's a humorist and not a comic, because a comic tells funny stories, but he just tells stories funny. What he seems to mean is that his success has come from talking about things that happen to himself and his friends. All his stories evolve from "something real that has happened to me — or almost happened."

Unlike myself and many other entertainers who sing or dance, Jerry did not have a burning desire to go into show business. Instead, his life was fairly normal. His family raised hogs and chickens for meat, had sweet potatoes and other farm goods. But his favorite food was French fries liberally covered with molasses.

Jerry had to milk the cows, tend the cattle, and keep fires burning in the wood stove and in the fireplace. He and his friends also enjoyed putting on their own rodeo, roping and riding the calves on the farm. They would also go coon and rabbit hunting, as well as playing "gator" or "Tarzan" in the nearby creek.

Much of Jerry's life in those years involved sports. He would listen to them on the radio and play them in school. After high school and a turn in the Navy, Jerry attended Mississippi Junior College and Mississippi State University and played football. Since that time he has been an active sports booster for his school, including being president of the Touchdown Club and Youth Baseball. He also claims

that when his children are playing, he is the loudest-mouthed parent in the stands.

Jerry was so slow in becoming a full-time entertainer that he worked for 18 years in the Mississippi Chemical Corporation, a firm manufacturing chemical plant foods. He was Director of Field Services when he began telling humorous stories as a way of more effectively training his sales staff. Eventually the story telling at work led to outside club dates and his first record album, "Jerry Clower From Yazoo City, Mississippi, Talkin'." A second album soon followed and now he has more than a dozen successful albums.

Jerry is an interesting man with a deep religious faith. He has worked as a lay preacher and is a deacon in the First Baptist Church of Yazoo City, Mississippi. He frequently works on behalf of the Gideons and was nominated by the state of Mississippi for the national 4-H Alumni Gold Key Award. When he went to ceremonies to receive that honor, he was one of eight people declared to be such a distinguished alumnus.

During the preparation of the chicken on the show, Jerry was separating the parts and mentioned the gizzard. When I was a little girl, my father used to threaten me when I did something wrong by saying that he was going to "beat the gizzard out of me." I spent a lot of time trying to determine which part of my body was the gizzard.

As many of you know, I have done commercials for Wesson Oil for many years. During the early work with them, one of the commercials required me to take a bite out of a chicken leg. The chicken, prepared with Wesson Oil, was delightfully crisp and tasty, actually making a loud crunching sound when I bit into a piece of it.

I would stand before the camera, singing, "The chicken's got a certain. . ." And then I would take a bite, smile, and finish with "Wesson-ality." Each time I did it, there was a loud crunch.

When you do commercials, the government is extremely serious about your not making false claims or doctoring the food in order to make it more appealing. There was a question about whether or not chicken fried in Wesson Oil could be that crispy. As a result, the advertising agency sent several representatives to see me. Fried chicken was made from Wesson Oil, then a bucket of chicken was taken into a recording studio where I had to stand before the microphone and bite into it in the same way I did on the ads. I would take a bite out of the chicken leg at the time I would musically. Then I had to sign an affidavit stating that the leg actually made such a crunchy sound.

The result was that the chicken did everything claimed. The advertising agency was able to show that the sound of the chicken was authentic, not electronically enhanced. However, I could not stop laughing at the absurdity of eating this huge tub full of chicken just to prove the sound it made when biting into it!

Jerry talked about using lard. When I was growing up, lard was used for just about everything imaginable. For example, when anyone got a case of bronchitis or the croup, Mother would heat up a mixture of lard and kerosene or coal oil. Then you would get it rubbed on your chest and back. We recovered very quickly, though we had to. There were 10 of us kids in the family and you smelled so bad that no one wanted to be around you!

Because Jerry is so big and such a good sport, we thought it would be fun to have an exercise segment when he appeared on my show. I showed him how to do some simple exercises that would tighten his stomach, but first I did a slight strip tease. Actually I had my exercise clothes underneath the dress I was wearing, but we had not warned Jerry what I was going to do. He was surprised and a little embarrassed, but a great sport.

Mississippi Fried Chicken

As Prepared by Jerry Clower

Ingredients:

1 Chicken
1 Cup Flour
Wesson Oil (Enough in
  Pan to Fry Chicken)
Salt to Taste
Pepper to Taste
(Brown Paper Bag)

Directions:

Cut chicken into pieces. Mix flour, salt to taste, pepper to taste in paper bag. Shake chicken chunks in bag to coat with flour mixture. Fry chicken pieces until done. Serve with sliced tomatoes, fried okra, butterbeans.

4-6 servings

Notes

Orville Redenbacher

Many people do not realize that Orville Redenbacher, the man behind such products as Orville Redenbacher Original Gourmet Popping Corn, is a real person, a pioneering researcher, humananitarian, and businessman. They think the name was created, like that of Betty Crocker, but he is both a real and extremely remarkable individual. He also has a great sense of humor and a mind that, at 80, is as sharp as that of much younger individuals.

Orville said that when he was a young man he used to run in track and field events as well as playing the Sousaphone. He said that those experiences taught him two lessons about life. One was that you have to stay out in front if you want to win. The other was that you have to toot your own horn, so that people will know about you.

Orville and I share some similarities of background. We're both Hoosiers and we both were active in the 4-H Club. But Orville's involvement with that organization continues to this day.

4-H relates to your heart, head, hands, and health. You dedicate your head to better thinking, your heart to greater loyalty, your hands to better service, and your health to better living. Orville followed this concept, staying connected with 4-H even while doing his pioneering research into popcorn hybridization at Purdue University.

The more successful Orville became, the more involved he was with 4-H, including forming a Junior 4-H Leadership Club, directing programs and camps, and participating on judging teams. He won the 4-H National Alumni

Recognition Award and, together with Beatrice/Hunt-Wesson, sponsors the 4-H Alumni Recognition Program on both local and national levels. He appears on public service television announcements and sponsors a special popcorn fund raiser. In fact, he has gone so far as to say that he owes his success to "A supportive network of family and friends, curiosity, common sense, stubbornness, tenacity, dreams, and 4-H."

I have not been as active with 4-H as Orville. However, I am proud to say that I was made a lifetime member of the organization, being given all the badges and medals you can earn.

Orville says that corn and popcorn can be traced back 5,600 years in history. But it was because of him that interest in the nutritious food has increased tremendously. Popcorn is now a billion dollar business and Orville has visited 96 nations, including two trips to the People's Republic of China and trips to Israel and South Africa, to help farmers breed corn and process popcorn.

Orville did not intend to dedicate his life to popcorn. In fact, his serious involvement in the industry was a major career change for him. He began his career as a high school vocational agriculture teacher. Then, for 12 years, he managed the 12,000 acre Princeton Farms in Princeton, Indiana, which specialized in purebred cattle and the production of hybrid corn seed and popcorn. He also was a county farm agent in Terre Haute during this period.

Orville's first business on his own was Chester, Inc., a partnership with Charles Bowman. The company's accomplishments included supplying the world with 30 percent of its hybrid popcorn seed. It was also during this period that he became interested in developing the special kernel that is the foundation for his popping corn.

Orville's great enthusiasm for life delighted me. He would flirt with all the women and, when the recipe he was making called for alcohol, he wanted to taste test the liquid to make certain it was right. Even more remarkable is that his wife, equally dynamic and loving, is older than he is.

The man's imagination never stops. He has created popcorn sculpture and popcorn stores featuring all manner of popcorn products. He was a fascinating guest and the song "Back Home Again in Indiana" was never sung with more fervor than when Orville and I (two dyed-in-the-wool Hoosiers) sang it on Country Kitchen!

Italian Chicken

As Prepared by Orville Redenbacher

Ingredients:

¼ Cup All-Purpose Flour
½ Tsp. Seasoned Salt
5 Chicken Breast Halves,
   Skinned, Boned & Pounded
   ½ Inch Thick
¼ Cup Orville Redenbacher's
   Popping & Topping Buttery
   Flavor Popcorn Oil
1 15-Oz. Can Hunt's
   Tomato Sauce Italian
½ Cup Chicken Broth
1 4½-Oz. Jar Sliced Mushrooms,
   Drained
½ Tsp. Garlic Powder
¼ Cup Grated Parmesan Cheese

Directions:

In dish combine flour and seasoned salt. Toss chicken breast halves in mixture to coat. Saute chicken in Orville Redenbacher's Popping & Topping Butter Flavor Popcorn Oil 3 to 4 minutes per side or until lightly browned.

Remove chicken to paper towel and drain fat from skillet. Add Hunt's Tomato Sauce Italian, chicken broth, sliced mushrooms, garlic powder and mix well. Bring sauce to boil, simmer, uncovered for three minutes.

Return chicken to pan and heat through. Sprinkle with grated parmesan cheese before serving.

5 servings

Notes

Jim Ed Brown

Jim Ed Brown began singing with the Grand Ole Opry when he was a small child in Sparkman, Arkansas. However, it would be several years later, not until 1959, that anyone connected with the Opry knew Jim Ed was singing with them. Prior to that his vocalizing was done at home with his sister, Maxine, as the two of them sat around a battery operated radio, dreaming of a career in the music business.

They learned words to those early songs from song books advertised to listeners of the Opry. It was later that Jim Ed and Maxine began writing their own work, including "Looking Back To See," their first hit.

The first professional appearances came when Jim Ed and Maxine began singing on KCLA Radio in Pine Bluff, Arkansas. From there they moved to the bigger station of KLRA Radio in Little Rock, a station that had a show called "Barnyard Frolic."

By 1954, Jim Ed, Maxine, Jim Reeves on rhythm guitar and Floyd Cramer on piano had recorded "Looking Back To See," a song rejected by most of the major labels. However, by chance the song was sung by the two Browns during an appearance on Ernest Tubb's Midnight Jamboree broadcast from Tubb's nationally known record store. A representative from Columbia Records heard their work, signed them to a contract, and that first song became a hit.

It was 1955 when Jim Ed and Maxine, along with their sister, Bonnie, joined with Red Foley and the Ozark Jubilee. That was followed by their signing with RCA Victor and, in 1959, recording "The Three Bells," their first million record hit.

Jim Ed is extremely respected in the music business. He's a man who is often called a "clutch player" or "money player." What this means is that he is able to deliver a fine performance even when he may not feel physically or emotionally at his best. He is also a man of great warmth and caring who, I suspect, was responsible for enabling me to appear on the Grand Ole Opry. The night I was on, he was the host for that segment, his kindness making the experience all the more rewarding.

I asked Jim Ed if he takes himself very seriously, he said that he takes his *work* seriously. He has learned what I have had to learn, to laugh at himself and not take himself too seriously, but to take what he *does* seriously.

Today Jim Ed works alone, his sisters having retired to spend more time with their families. He has his own show on The Nashville Network and has played throughout the world, including recording in Japanese. His work is so popular that every song he has recorded has made the charts, including, "You Don't Bring Me Flowers," "Lying In Love With You," "Fools," "If The World Ran Out Of Love Tonight," and so many others.

Jim Ed and I talked about men who cook. My father was a wonderful cook who could cook anything and taught my mother. Historically, many of the great cooks and chefs have been men. For example, when I'm in Nashville for my show, I stay at the Sheraton Music City where the kitchen is presided over by Chef Jeff. He has given me a tour of the complex kitchen which is extremely clean, well organized, and the source of some wonderful meals. When you have to be on the road and away from home, it becomes important whether the place where you stay is clean, comfortable, and makes you feel welcome. At times entertainers have had a bad reputation with hotels and all of us have suffered for it. The Sheraton Music City treats everyone with respect, truly giving us a home away from home.

Jim Ed is a hunter and the duck dish he made was one of the most ambitious we have had on the show. You can use tame or wild duck for the recipe, though I was surprised to learn that the only difference in the preparation was adding a bay leaf.

Wild Duck Casserole

As Prepared by Jim Ed Brown

Ingredients:

3 Wild Ducks or
   1-2 Domestic Ducks
1 Onion, Sliced
2 Carrot Sticks
1 Apple, Halved
½ Cup Chopped Onion
4 Celery Ribs
½ Cup Butter
¼ Cup Flour
1 6-Oz Can Sliced Mushrooms
1½ Cups Milk
1 Tsp. Chopped Parsley
1½ Tsp. Pepper
½ Tsp. Salt
1 Pkg. Wild, Long-Grain Rice,
   8 Oz., Cooked
1 Pkg. Slivered Almonds, 2½ Oz.

Directions:

Boil ducks until tender with sliced onion, celery ribs, carrot sticks, and halved apple. Let cool 1 hour and de-bone ducks.

Prepare rice according to instructions on bag. Preheat oven to 350°. In a deep skillet melt butter, then saute chopped onion. Stir in flour. Add sliced mushrooms and their liquid, then add milk, parsley, salt and pepper. Add contents of saucepan to cooked rice. Add chunks of de-boned duck to the other ingredients, place all in a greased, 2-quart casserole. Sprinkle with almonds and bake at 350° for about 30 minutes.

2-3 servings

Notes

Jimmy Dean

immy Dean, one of the most outrageous guests I've ever had on my show, was raised in a manner that was quite similar to my own. We were both raised in poverty and often humiliated by our experiences as children. Yet instead of being defeated by the teasing of our more affluent playmates, we were spurred on to make something better of ourselves. My poverty stimulated me to do better, to have better things, to live better. Jimmy Dean said virtually the same thing, that when the other kids made fun of him and laughed at him, it didn't do anything but light a fire under him, and I kind of felt the same way.

Jimmy told me, "Poverty was the greatest motivating factor in my life. When other people laughed at the house I lived in, the clothes I wore, and when they laughed at my mother because she cut hair, all they did was build a fire under me. And I said then, 'One way or the other, I'll come back to this town some day and I'll show you I'm as good as you are.' "

Jimmy was born in Plainview, Texas, on a farm that was dirt poor even before the Depression hit the following year. He jokingly commented to me, "I used to think the only reason they brought me through when I was a baby was that they needed another hand!"

Jimmy had little time for play in those early years. He told me his family was so poor, that his mother had him pulling a cotton sack when he was six. Eventually he had to dig ditches, run tractors, clean chicken coops, bale hay,

and like all farm kids, when no one was looking, steal watermelons.

I talked with Jimmy about how much money he has now. He does have tremendous personal wealth, both from his success as an entertainer and from his Jimmy Dean sausage company. However, he downgrades the importance of money, saying that, "Wealth and success, to me, are a state of mind. My granddaddy was the wealthiest and most successful man I ever knew, and I doubt that he ever made $10,000 a year in his life. But he was the best farmer in Hale County. He knew that. And his barn was redder and his house was whiter. He raised nine kids and he had a marvelous relationship with the Man upstairs. Now if you want to talk success and wealth, that's it."

Then, after being philosophical for a moment, he grinned and admitted, "Yes, I've got a few dollars." How much money is that Jimmy? "Well, for Christmas, I bought my dog a boy."

One of Jimmy Dean's great loves is music, though he was older than many of us who knew we wanted to be professional from the time we were small children. After entering the Air Force at age 18, he discovered he was a natural entertainer, singing and telling humorous stories.

Jimmy got his start when a small group of friends playing in a Washington, D.C. club, had one of their members take sick. They all knew that Jimmy carried an accordion with him everywhere, playing for his own amusement. They felt he was skilled enough and asked if he would substitute. They weren't paid, though they split whatever tips they might receive. Since he was broke, he decided to give it a try, liked it, and started a major career in show business.

Even today, Jimmy plays to relax, not just to entertain. When we were at the Sheraton Music City in Nashville, every night he would go to the lounge to play the piano and sing. He also fell victim to what he described as a "Vodka Front" that seemed to move through the lounge whenever he was there. After falling prey to one such

"assault," he went into the lobby where he noticed a large grandfather clock. Not realizing what he was seeing, he opened the cabinet and tried to climb inside in order to call home!

Jimmy Dean claims that the following recipe originated with his Aunt Versie, a woman he describes as being "a religious cook . . . Everything she puts out is either a burnt offering or a sacrifice." In reality, it was developed in the Jimmy Dean kitchens in Dallas where a skilled staff regularly develops tasty new recipes for their sausage.

Fall-Baked Apples

As Prepared by Jimmy Dean

Ingredients:

4 Large Cooking Apples
4 Tbsp. Minced Onions
1 Lb. Jimmy Dean Special
   Recipe Sausage
1 Cup Bread Crumbs
½ Cup Brown Sugar
¼ Tsp. Cinnamon

Directions:

Preheat oven to 350°, and butter a shallow pan. Cut a slice from the top of apples. Scoop out core and pulp, leaving shells ¾ inches thick.

Chop the pulp and combine it and the minced onion with the sausage. Saute the sausage mixture, breaking the meat with a fork, cooking until the rawness disappears. Mix in bread crumbs.

Sprinkle the apple shells with half the brown sugar and cinnamon. Stuff firmly with sausage mixture. Sprinkle with the remaining sugar and cinnamon. Bake for 40 minutes or until apples are tender.

4 servings

Notes

Michael Johnson

I first learned about Michael Johnson seven or eight years ago when I was putting together a new act. There was a man named Mike Post, a songwriter whose theme music for shows such as "The Rockford Files" and "Hill Street Blues," among others, is familiar to most of us, who was also writing for me. As we talked, he mentioned an extremely talented young man from Minneapolis named Michael Johnson who had a song called "Bluer Than Blue."

My first reaction was surprise. The music industry is so concentrated in Nashville, Los Angeles, and New York that I never thought about serious recording artists living in Minneapolis. But the song "Bluer Than Blue" quickly became a part of my act. I sang a blues medley, and when I got to "Bluer Than Blue," I would get up on the piano while wearing a big, beautiful boa and then sing the song. Thus this man I had never met, from a city outside the mainstream of recording, immediately influenced my work.

Michael began his musical training with his older brother, Paul, when he was 13 years old. They taught themselves the rudiments of guitar, Michael constantly listening to rock, jazz, and classical guitarists in order to master, then adapt the methods of others to his own playing.

Michael told me that the greatest influence during those early years was a nun in his parochial school, a woman he adored. She encouraged him repeatedly, a situation similar to one I experienced when growing up.

In my case, it was Sister Mary William, a beautiful woman, who was the organist at St. Bernard's Church when I was young. She played an old pump organ and she would have me sit next to her, pumping the pedals while she played. She was also the one who put me in the big choir when I was still in elementary school, getting me to sing two masses every Sunday. It was wonderful training for a singer.

By the time Michael was in college, he won a contract with Epic Records as a part of a contest. He was able to go on the road, performing in colleges and clubs. Then, at 21, he had formal training with classical guitarist Graciano Tarrago in Bacelona.

When Michael returned to the United States, he spent a year touring with the Chad Mitchell Trio. He told me that another aspiring song writer/singer in the group was a man named John Denver.

The touring period was extraordinarily hectic, the group performing 191 concerts that year. Michael said that in any city where they had friends, they would leave their laundry in airport lockers. Their friends would wash it and they would pick it up on the way out of town.

Since that period, Michael has had great success. There was "Bluer Than Blue," the song that introduced me to his work, "Almost Like Being In Love," "This Night Won't Last Forever," and "Give Me Wings," among others. His work frequently has a sound that makes it popular on radio formats that include Country, Top 40, Adult Contemporary, and even Rhythm and Blues. He is extremely versatile and travels widely from his rather unusual, for a singer/song writer, home base of Minneapolis.

Michael brought a recipe his wife, Sally, prepared, though he obviously had mastered cooking it himself. One tangent of our conversation while cooking was about "toe jam," definitely *not* a product of his meal or any meal you would ever want to eat. It is a term familiar mostly to farm kids.

When we were growing up, we lacked most forms of plumbing and had no washtub. Baths were literally only on Saturdays, a time when my mother would laboriously fill containers of water, heat them on the old wood burning stove, then go through the cleansing ritual. Since there were 10 of us kids, this was an elaborate production.

But during the week we were often barefoot and, in summer, the ground would be so soft that dirt would get between our toes. We called the mud "toe jam" and constantly threatened to make each other a "toe jam sandwich." Fortunately, Michael's recipe had nothing to do with such childish experiences.

Chili Beef Stir-Fry

As Prepared by Michael Johnson

Ingredients:

¼ Cup Wesson Oil
2 Tbsp. Soy Sauce
1 Clove Minced Garlic
6 Grinds Fresh Black Pepper
2 Tsp. Chili Paste w/Garlic
1 Tbsp. Peanut Oil
1 Lb. Top Round, Cut in Slices
   against Grain ¼" x 1" x 2"
1 Tbsp. Minced Ginger
1 Cup Julienned Carrots
   ¼" x ¼" x 2"
2 Cups Cleaned Pea Pods
½ Cup Water or Unsalted
   Chicken or Beef Stock
1 Tbsp. Corn Starch
½ Cup Green Onions (Cut on
   Diagonal into 1/3" Slices)
1 Tbsp. Toasted Sesame Seeds

Directions:

To make marinade: Whisk together in large bowl, ¼ cup vegetable oil, 2 tbsp. soy sauce, 1 clove minced garlic, 6 grinds fresh black pepper, and 1 tsp. chili paste with garlic. Toss 1 lb. sliced top round in marinade and cover with plastic, refrigerate 2-3 hours (toss twice during 2-3 hours).

Heat 1 tbsp. peanut oil in large saute pan or wok on high (not smoking). Toss meat once more and add to oil (without extra marinade). Toss meat and cook quickly until color turns. Add 1 tbsp. minced ginger, carrots and pea pods, tossing between each ingredient. Cook approximately 2 more minutes (no more than 5 minutes total time). (Vegetables should be crisp & tender & meat medium rare to medium).

Combine ½ cup water, 1 tbsp. cornstarch, and 1 tsp. of chili paste with garlic in small bowl. Turn heat to low, add cornstarch mixture. Stir & cook just long enough to form a light sauce. Serve with white rice (4 portions). Garnish with ½ cup sliced green onions and 1 tbsp. toasted sesame seeds.

4 servings

Notes

Johnny Tillotson

ohnny Tillotson reminded me of the first time he had seen me in public. It was many years ago in New York City's Pennsylvania Station. I was there because I was a part of the touring company of "The Sound Of Music."

The night before, I had given a performance that was extremely memorable for me. There were critics there, Richard Rodgers, his wife, Dorothy, and Mary Martin who had played the role before me.

The opening of "Sound Of Music" required me to climb onto a prop tree, then be wheeled onto the stage. I stepped down from the tree and had to sing "The hills are alive with the sound of music. . ." at the top of my voice. There was no time to get control of my nerves, and I am always on edge just before a performance. There was no way either to get a feel for the theater to be certain you are using your voice properly for the audience. Mary Martin told me that she always hated that moment in the show until that night when she saw me do it and realized that the approach, though rough on the singer, was extremely effective for the audience.

The next day I was leaving for Detroit to open what proved to be the most successful touring company of that show or any show for that matter. I traveled with Barbara, my 4 year old daughter, and Joseph, who was just a few months old. The tour lasted 15 months and I was helped by my nanny, Emily Maude Dare. She was a woman who loved my children almost as much as I did, a tremendous help. Yet during that morning at Penn Station, I had no

idea that Johnny Tillotson was watching me, and certainly no idea that he would one day be on my television show.

Johnny's career has actually had two strong periods. He is a successful star today, but he had his first successes in the 1950's. He had decided to become a professional singer by the time he was 9 and living in Palatka, Florida. His parents took him seriously, bought him a guitar, and, by the time he entered Palatka Sr. High, he had his own professional band. From there he appeared on a local Jacksonville, Florida, program called the "Toby Dowdy Show." And when Toby Dowdy went off the air, Johnny was given his own show.

Johnny's interests were varied so, in 1955, he entered the University of Florida to study journalism, radio, and television. He had his degree by 1959 but also some unusual experiences. He was one of the six national winners in the 1957 Pet Milk Talent Contest, going to Nashville where his singing impressed a local music publisher. This led to his being asked to record for Cadence Records whose singers then included such names as the Chordettes, Andy Williams, and the Everly Brothers. That first record, "Dreamy Eyes," made it to the top of the charts in numerous cities throughout the country. It was followed by "Poetry In Motion," a #1 hit on the charts internationally.

During those college years, Johnny frequently needed a manager to represent him. In the music business, managers and agents are used to make contacts with club owners, record company executives and others in order to help you get work. A new singer seldom can get a manager interested in handling the act because there are too many unknown factors about the person's potential. Yet without a manager, it is often difficult to get work.

Johnny's answer was to become his own manager. He would call, pretend to be a professional representing this exciting new singer, then book himself into the club. Then, as he began appearing at more and more places, people did like what they heard and started calling him.

The biggest break came in 1962 when Johnny recorded both a single and an album called "It Keeps Right On A-Hurtin." Not only was it one of his biggest selling songs, it also was one of the first records in the country to be called a "cross-over." This meant that it was played both on pop and country stations, hitting both charts. Of course, it also contained such well known songs as "I'm So Lonesome I Could Cry," "Send Me The Pillow That You Dream On," "I Can't Help It," and "Funny How Time Slips Away." "It Keeps Right On A-Hurtin" earned a Grammy nomination for the Best Country Song Of The Year and was recorded by 108 stars ranging from Elvis Presley to Dean Martin and Eddy Arnold.

There were numerous other successes as well, such as his creating the theme song for the television series, "Gidget," starring Sally Fields. He then moved into night club work, strengthening his appeal nationwide.

Today Johnny Tillotson is extremely popular, playing both his older songs and the new ones he keeps producing. Many of the younger people who hear his music learn of it first through their parents playing it. "A lot of the younger generation gets initiated into my music because their mothers play it on the stereo at home." However, he jokes that the one reason his daughter, Kelli, delighted in his singing when she was a teenager was because it ensured that there would be enough money to pay for Duran Duran albums!

Salmon with Lemon Basil Sauce

As Prepared by Johnny Tillotson

Ingredients:

4 Salmon Steaks, 1 Inch Thick
1 Tsp. Minced Garlic
½ Cup Lemon Juice
2 Dashes Tabasco
¼ Tsp. Dry Mustard
½ Tsp. Salt
½ Tsp. Sugar
1 Tsp. Worcestershire Sauce
1 Tsp. White Vinegar
½ Cup Unsalted Butter
*½ Cup Coarsely Chopped
  Fresh Basil*
2 Lemon Peels, Grated
¼ Cup Wesson Oil
¼ Cup Minced Shallots

Directions:

Combine minced shallots, minced garlic, lemon juice, Tabasco, dry mustard, salt, sugar, Worcestershire sauce, and white vinegar. Simmer at a gentle boil over medium heat until mixture is reduced by about one third. Add unsalted butter, lemon peels, and basil. Heat until butter is melted.

Brush the salmon steaks with oil and grill 7 minutes on the first side, then about 5-7 minutes on the second side. Spoon sauce over salmon steaks and serve.

*This sauce can be used with any fleshy fish steak.

4-6 servings

Notes

T.G. Sheppard

T.G. Sheppard was an overnight sensation. In 1975, on the Melodyland label, he recorded "Devil In The Bottle" which raced to the top of the charts. It was a shock to everyone in the industry because so few artists achieve such instant success. Of course, the success of T.G. Sheppard was no surprise to Bill Browder who had previously spent many years working towards the moment when T.G. Sheppard would triumph. And since Bill Browder is the real name of T.G. Sheppard, the story does become rather complicated.

Bill Browder was raised in Humbolt, Tennessee, where he was exposed to both country and gospel music in equally heavy doses. He began playing the guitar and saxophone, his first success coming when he played for the Travis Womack Band in Memphis. He managed to gain a record contract with Sonic, producing such best forgotten singles as "Little Girl Next Door."

Soon Bill Browder "disappeared" and Brian Stacy became the name he used when he became the opening act for the Beach Boys and Jan & Dean. He recorded again, this time achieving some popularity with the song "High School Days."

Several things happened around the same time. T.G. married, he entered the field of record distribution, and he became friends with Elvis Presley, a man who helped give him a better perspective of life as an entertainer.

"I first met Elvis right after he got out of the service in 1961 and my wife, Diana, and I spent many hours with him as friends. Elvis taught me a great deal about life, and among the lessons that stayed with me are that money is not the most important thing in life, and life has no meaning unless you have someone to share it with. Having a good home and keeping it intact is worth more than all the material things one could have."

By 1974, when Bill Browder had formally become T.G. Sheppard, he was firmly based in the music business. He formed his own production company, learning marketing and merchandising, as well as singing. Then, after his first hit under his new name, he followed up with "Tryin' To Beat The Morning Home" which he co-wrote. By 1976, Cash Box Magazine named him "Best New Male Artist." And from then on, hits became a way of life.

The "overnight success" now says, "I'm not as naive as I was when I first started out. It takes time to become good at your craft—something I didn't realize in the beginning. But if fame does come overnight, it goes overnight. And what I've learned throughout my years in this business is that if you build a strong foundation, if you don't burn your bridges along the way, if you're basically kind to people, if you stay level-headed and take your music and your business seriously, and if you can contribute to the industry— then I believe you'll be able to last a while."

One of the results of T.G.'s success is his bus. He cooks on his bus and brought the bus to the studio where I saw it. What amazed me is that the bus is nicer than many apartments. It has color television, full stereo, two floors, and is very much like a mansion on wheels. I suppose that when you're on the road so much, you need something that is a consistent home.

During the cooking segment, T.G. was singing the song from "The Brady Bunch," which surprised me. I'm always amazed at how popular that show was. I was once on a show in Nashville where the entire audience sang the words just before my appearance.

T.G. asked me about Alice who was the housekeeper character. Ann B. Davis who played Alice and I were always so busy with the show that, for five years, we seldom had time to cook for our own families. She and I used to delight in all the scenes where we were in the kitchen, stirring something for dinner, since our real lives seldom allowed us time for such tasks.

T.G. and I both have similar acts when we are on the road. We both like to entertain, provide a little comedy, a little music, and a well planned program.

Road shows where you are entertaining in clubs, halls, and the like, are wonderful experiences, though extremely costly. You need to hire arrangers to constantly update your act; you have musicians, and all manner of support people who must accompany you. At the same time, such shows bring you closer to your audience and are an experience that transcends anything you might earn. As T.G. explained it:

"I have fun at my shows, but if it ever came to the point where I had to walk onstage just to get paid, well, that's the time to move on. People ask me what I look forward to after a show and I tell them 'getting back out there and doing it again.' Good records lead to major concerts, and of course, the third important step is television."

Considering how far T.G. has come, it is obvious that whatever he goes after will prove successful for him.

Chicken and Shrimp Supreme

As Prepared by T.G. Sheppard

Ingredients:

¼ Cup Butter
½ Lb. Sliced Fresh
  Mushrooms
2 Tbsp. Sliced Scallions
2 Cans Condensed Cream of
  Chicken Soup, 10¾ Oz.
½ Cup Sherry
½ Cup Light Cream or Half
  and Half
1 Cup (4 Oz.) Shredded
  Cheddar Cheese
2 Cups Diced Cooked Chicken
2 Cups Cooked Shrimp
  (Cleaned, Peeled)
2 Tbsp. Chopped Parsley
Hot Buttered Rice, Approx. 8 Oz.

Directions:

Melt butter in a 3-quart saucepan over low heat. Add sliced fresh mushrooms and sliced scallions. Add condensed cream of chicken soup. Gradually stir in sherry, then half and half or cream. Add shredded cheddar cheese and heat over low heat, stirring occasionally until cheese melts. Add diced cooked chicken, cooked and cleaned shrimp.

Heat to serving temperature, but do not boil. Just before serving, stir in chopped parsley. Serve over hot buttered rice.

4 servings

Notes

Sharon White

Sharon White is part of the White Family whom I had on the show at another time. She is married to entertainer Ricky Skaggs, and they have an extremely strong relationship in which they each consider the other their best friend. This is Ricky's second marriage, and he told me he has reduced the number of days he is on the road so that the two of them can spend more time together and with their daughter, Molly Kate.

Sharon began singing with her sister, Cheryl, and their father, Buck, in 1967. "We'd sit down and play for hours every night," said Sharon. "Our harmonies were influenced by a lot of bluegrass singers, but we always had more of a softer blend, a mellow sound. We've always had this little bounce or swing to our music, even on slow songs.

The family moved to Nashville in 1971. They had played at Bill Monroe's Beanblossom Festival that year, an experience that kindled her desire to be regularly on stage. "We played on stage as a guest act. It was like building a fire under me and Cheryl. It started a flame we couldn't put out."

Sharon is one of these people who probably doesn't have a mean bone in her body. She is a gentle young woman who is a wonderful daughter, sister, wife, mother, and friend. "People tell us we look so happy. Well, we are happy. How could we not be? It's very fulfilling. We thank God every day. That's the blessing; that's the success."

Many of the recipes Sharon knows came from her mother-in-law, Dorothy Skaggs. Sharon even brought me some sauerkraut that Dorothy had canned, a skill that is becoming a lost art. My sisters who still live in Indiana and Kentucky still do canning each year, just as our mother did. It's a valuable skill and something I do miss.

Sharon talked about visualization as a reason for part of her success. She said that she feels that if you can picture yourself doing something, then you can achieve it.

I believe that, too. We too often make assumptions that

we will fail at something when, in reality, there is no reason we cannot achieve it. By picturing ourselves having the success, career, happiness, or whatever positive goal we seek, there is no reason why it should escape our grasp.

Sharon is now facing the problem of traveling with a new baby. You spend so much energy performing, you fear you will short change the baby. At the same time, it is such a pleasure to have the child on the road that you are concerned when you don't. Then, when your child reaches school age, you are torn about what to do because you want your child to have a stable education and you also don't want to miss the time growing up.

Molly Kate is already a ham and well adjusted to the travel. I suspect that there will come a day when Sharon and Ricky's daughter will join her mother's act. She is adorable and the type of child I suspect will want to be with them.

FOOD FACTS

Three types of fruit have their seeds on the outside. They are raspberries, strawberries, and blackberries.

●

It takes 540 peanuts to make a jar of peanut butter.

●

Peanuts are not true nuts — they really belong to the same family as dry beans, split peas and lentils.

●

The most nutritious meat available, recommended by doctors for patients in low calorie and low sodium diets is —Rabbit.

Pork 'n' Kraut

As Prepared by Sharon White

Ingredients:

*2 Lbs. Pork Loin,
   Sliced in 2" Strips
1 Lg. Can of Sauerkraut
6 Med. Potatoes, Sliced Thick
3 Med. Yellow Onions, Sliced
6 Carrots,
   Peeled and Sliced Lengthwise
3 Tbsp. Wesson Oil
Salt
Pepper*

Directions:

Slice pork loin into 2″ slices. Slice potatoes thickly. Slice yellow onions. Peel and slice carrots lengthwise. Brown pork in oil with salt and pepper to taste over med./low heat.

Place all of the pork in bottom of dutch oven, then a layer of sauerkraut, a layer of potatoes, onions, and carrots, then layer vegetables until all ingredients are used. Pour juice from sauerkraut can over all of it, add water if necessary. Cover and simmer until done; approximately 1 hour.

4-6 servings

Notes

Dan Seals

Dan Seals told me that he was raised a little like the Waltons but in a three room house which was part of an army barracks in an oil producing area of West Texas. There were the grandparents, the parents, Dan and his brother all cramped together. Now, being one of ten children, I know what it was like to sleep four in a bed, but even with only two children, Dan's family was almost as crowded as mine.

Coming from that type of background, it is odd experiencing what many people consider a "normal" night's sleep. I never slept alone in a bed until I went to New York, and then I had some difficulty getting used to the experience. With so many kids in one bed, it was common to awaken with someone's toe jammed against your nose, yet that physical closeness of all the bodies became familiar. In addition, whenever there was an unusually cold night, the pile of bodies in the bed generated comforting heat.

Dan started singing very young. He was four years old when he, his brother, and his father began entertaining. His brother, who was nine, was a state champion musician in his age group and somewhat of a celebrity in West Texas. As a result, Dan, who played the standing-up bass, received quite a bit of attention from the start. In fact, Dan's brother is well known for his work as half of the duet of Seals and Croft.

Dan's first musical career as a professional came when he teamed with John Ford Coley. He was calling himself "England Dan" Seals during that period, his music being pop, not country. The two became well known for such

hits as "I'd Really Love To See You Tonight," "Love Is The Answer," and "Nights Are Forever."

Despite calling himself "England Dan," his roots were Middle Tennessee where his great, great grandparents farmed land near Dickson, Sylvia, and Big Sandy in the 1700's. During that period, his great, great uncle played the fiddle in dances held in an area that is now called David Allen Coe's Ruskin Cave. His grandfather eventually had his own band in that same cave, though he resettled in Texas because Tennessee farming was not providing an adequate living. By the time Dan was growing up, the men in the Seals family worked the oil fields by day and played music at night.

The earliest song Dan learned was "Don't Let The Stars Get In Your Eyes," a big hit for Perry Como. But most of the music he enjoyed was country. For example, I can still remember back to being a small child and singing "She'll Be Coming Around The Mountain," "In The Blue Ridge Mountains of Virginia," and "On The Trail Of The Lonesome Pine."

Eventually Dan returned to those roots. As he has commented, "I like pop music, but I love country music. It comes from inside."

Ironically, it was pop music that brought Dan to Nashville. He and his partner used a studio just outside the country music capital, a studio he still uses now that he is performing as a solo country singer.

The change to country was well received. Dan's first album, "Rebel Heart," had several successful songs, including "God Must Be A Cowboy," a Top Ten hit.

Dan and I talked about the corn bread he made with his soup. For those of us who grew up in the South and Midwest, corn bread was a staple of our diets. The corn is extremely nourishing and the bread is quite filling, even when poverty prevents you from having anything else to eat.

The taste of corn bread can be changed readily as well. One treat we enjoyed, even though we got it when there was no other food in the house, was a combination of corn bread and milk to make a mush. If you added salt to the mixture, it became a main dish. If you added sugar, the sweetness changed it just enough so it was a wonderful dessert. In its original form, though, corn bread was the perfect accompaniment for Dan's delicious soup.

Homestyle Potato Soup
As Prepared by Dan Seals

Ingredients:

2 Med. Onions, Chopped
3-4 Chopped Carrots
3 Ribs of Celery, Chopped
8 Potatoes, Med., Cut into
  Chunks with Skin left on
Salt
Pepper
2 Bay Leaves
1 Tsp. Sweet Basil
1½ Cups Dry Milk (Nonfat)
1 Stick Butter (½ Cup)
Parsley

Directions:

Cut potatoes into chunks with skin left on, and add to ½ gallon boiling water with 2 tbsp. salt. Saute in butter: carrots, celery, onions, bay leaves and basil. Add sauteed vegetables to boiling potatoes and add 1 tbsp. pcppcr.

Cook over med. heat for 30 minutes or until potatoes are tender. Remove pot from heat, let cool 5 minutes. Add butter to pot and then slowly add 1½ cups nonfat dry milk, stirring constantly. (Make sure soup is not hot enough to curdle milk when it is added.) Reheat soup to serve, sprinkle with parsley.

8 servings

Notes

Sylvia

Sylvia is an unusual young woman in show business. She was only 29 when she was on my show, yet she had the drive, determination, and realistic attitude towards the business that normally will be found in someone much older.

The oldest of three children, Sylvia was shy, somewhat withdrawn, yet she had a strong sense of where she wanted to be. At three, she sang for the first time in the Kokomo, Indiana Pilgrim Holiness Church. However, she did not spend her time trying to perform. Instead, she attempted to learn the music business.

For many years Sylvia listened to country music on the radio and tried to draw portraits of the stars. Although extremely pretty, she said, "As a teenager, I didn't date at all. I preferred staying at home and listening to the radio. When the disc jockeys would drop bits of insider talk—like so-and-so just finished such-and-such a record—I'd write it all down. That was just part of the educational process I felt was necessary before heading to Nashville."

Oddly, the first country music star Sylvia met in person—Dolly Parton—she met in a different Nashville—Nashville, Indiana. She brought a portrait of Dolly she had drawn and was invited to come on board the star's tour bus. Instead of gushing how much she loved Dolly's work, Sylvia had the maturity to ask Dolly how she got started in the business. As Sylvia recalls, Parton explained all the problems, then said, "...if you want it, don't let anything stop you. Make up your mind, work real hard, and you'll do it."

Part of that preparation went beyond learning to sing and learning about the business. Sylvia also trained to become a secretary so she would have skills to offer potential employers. She knew she would have to work for a living until her singing skills were recognized. As a result, she was able to get a job with producer Tom Collins, a job that brought her into contact with the major singers of country music.

For 4½ years Sylvia worked for Collins, always developing her skills as a singer. "I've always been a dreamer, yet I've always had a strong sense of just who I am and where I'm going," Sylvia explained to me. "It was all of that which prepared me for Nashville, took me there, and set my dreams in motion."

Sylvia did have one break, though. Her first record contract, with RCA, resulted in two singles on the Top 40 charts. Then, when she recorded "Tumbleweed," she made it to the Top 10. Finally, in the fall of 1979, Sylvia soloed on the Canadian tour of Charlie Pride. Since then she has worked with numerous country music stars.

The success of any entertainer making appearances is determined, in part, by the number of days per year that they are able to work. By 1981, Sylvia was on the road for 323 working days. She traveled by car, not having her own band or back-up. She worked with a different set of musicians every night, never knowing quite what to expect.

Most of the dates were in small, isolated towns as Sylvia paid her dues by singing anywhere people wanted to hear her. Word of her skill was reaching top people in the record industry and one executive told her he would fly in to hear her wherever she was playing. He thought better of the idea when he learned that most of her shows were in towns too small to have an airport and too isolated to easily drive from the nearest big city. As a result, it took him a month before he could find Sylvia in a community located where it would be accessible.

Now Sylvia has her own group and is playing the bigger clubs. But she does not regret the earlier pressures. As she explained:

"I hear a lot of entertainers complaining about how hard they work, but I think that's just *bull*! Darn right I work hard and so does my band. That's our job. But we also have fun while we're working. It's a privilege to be allowed in to entertain people and you have to work hard to *earn* that privilege."

By 1982, Sylvia had found true success. Her song, "Drifter," became #1 on the charts, followed by the million seller "Nobody" and the album, "Just Sylvia," going gold. She began appearing on television on programs ranging from "Merv Griffin" to "Solid Gold" and "American Bandstand."

"Eventually I'd like to act in film. I've been offered a couple of things, but I don't want to be just a singer plugged into a plot. I want a real role."

In the meantime, she also starred in our kitchen. Her recipe for spaghetti was delicious.

Spaghetti

As Prepared by Sylvia

Ingredients:

2 Lbs. Ground Round
2 Med. Onions, Chopped
Instant Minced Garlic,
*   1 Tsp. or to Taste*
Dried Crushed Red Pepper,
*   ¼ Tsp. or to Taste*
Italian Herb Seasoning,
*   1 Tsp. or to Taste*
2 Lg. Jars Chunky Garden Style
*   Spaghetti Sauce*
½ Cup Red Cooking Wine
½ Cup Honey
1 16-Oz. Pkg. Vermicelli

Directions:

Chop onions. Brown meat with garlic, red pepper, and Italian herb seasoning. Drain meat. Add onions and wine, simmer 5-10 minutes.

In large pot 8-10 inches deep, combine meat and spaghetti sauce. Simmer, adjust spices to taste. Add honey. Cook 1-1½ hours. Cook vermicelli according to package just before serving.

4-6 servings

My par
were hor
behind c
then, no
inferenc
dishones
She wen
dressed
few wor
backwar
his white
compost
Hoyt's
to San Fr
singer or
back Dol
Trio reco
World" b
Numerou
other sin
on his alu
I think
a guest w
their favc
when cor
recipes tl
and cook
favorite r
was for v
vored wit
While
admit tha

eral days. We got to raft down the river and slept in a cabin way out in the wilds of Idaho. I wouldn't sleep on the ground, though if I had, I'd have seen more of stars so big, it was as though you could reach out and touch them. You could only get to his place by airplane or horseback, the quiet being extremely peaceful after the harried pace of New York and other big cities where I worked.

There was one night when I kept hearing a strange noise. The cabin was little more than a shelter from bad weather so I thought it was the building that I heard. Then I realized that the sound was coming from a box in the corner, a box that was a home to a family of mice.

A day or two later, my daughter came running, screaming into the cabin. I looked out the door and there was a procession of four long snakes passing by, looking like a small train in a hurry to get to its destination.

I may have been raised in the country, but I would have been uncomfortable living around mice and snakes on a farm. Out there in the wilderness, all I wanted was a quick way back to civilization.

Carol Burnett says that her idea of "roughing it" is room service and two TV channels. I'm not quite that bad, but I can relate to the idea that every wilderness experience should still include nights in a good hotel.

As much as I do not like camping, I'm not certain I wouldn't have put success in the same category had I known what it would be like. I got the role working on "The Brady Bunch" when my kids were fairly young and few people ever recognized me on the street. Once it was a hit, we found that we could no longer go to Disneyland or Sea World or any large amusement area. People would be all over me, wanting to talk, to get autographs for their child-

ren, and my children didn't know how to take that. They were being denied their special time and felt it was not fair.

I remember one time when my daughter, Lizzie, and I were in Central Park and all these kids came running up saying, "Oh, Mrs. Brady! Mrs. Brady!" As it happened, Lizzie began tugging at my skirt and said, "Tell them that we're your *real* kids."

Thank God my children have become fantastic adults and good friends. I know it must have been difficult to have grown up being "Mrs. Brady's" real children.

John believes in eating extremely healthy foods. He said that part of his good health comes from being "high" all the time and he did not mean on drugs. He meant that he is literally high—his home is 8,500 feet above sea level in the Rocky Mountains.

John and his wife, Kay, have six children and their lifestyle makes things extremely difficult for both of them. He is frequently traveling in order to earn his living, something that upsets his kids because he is so frequently away. What is sad is that there are so many ways to earn a living and some of them, such as entertaining, require sacrifices which prevent us from fully enjoying our kids' growing up years even as we are working so they can have some pleasures. This is especially hard on the wives of entertainers who often must function as both mother and father, an extremely difficult role.

Nitty Gritty Dirt Chicken

As Prepared by John McEuen

Ingredients:

1 Chicken, Cut into
   Conventional Pieces, Skinned
1½ Cups Flour
¼ Tsp. Cayenne Pepper
½ Tsp. Paprika
2 Tbsp. Pot Herbs*
½ Tsp. Garlic Powder
¼ Tsp. Pepper
Wesson Oil
   (½ inch deep in frying pan)
Shortening
   (to coat Dutch Oven)
4 Potatoes, Sliced (Round)
4 Carrots, Sliced
1 Onion, Sliced (into Rings)

*POT HERBS:

2 Tsp. Parsley Flakes
1 Tsp. Onion Flakes
1 Tsp. Garlic Flakes
1 Tsp. Basil
1 Tsp. Thyme
1 Bay Leaf

Directions:

Mix flour, cayenne pepper, paprika, 1 tbsp. pot herbs, garlic powder and pepper to make breading. Roll chicken in flour mixture. Brown in oil ½ inch deep in frying pan.

Heat oven to 375° F. Coat Dutch Oven with shortening. Place chicken in Dutch Oven, large pieces on bottom, smaller on top. Add 4 sliced potatoes, 4 sliced carrots, 1 sliced onion to top of chicken. Sprinkle 1 tbsp. pot herbs over vegetables.

Cook covered at 375° F 45 minutes to 1 hour. Serve with steamed broccoli.

4-6 servings

Notes

Bobby Bare

obby Bare was typical of so many serious entertainers. He had promised to be on my show, then his wife unexpectedly took ill and had to go to the hospital. Instead of canceling, he went to the hospital, made sure she would be all right, stayed with her until he needed to be in the studio, then brought his teenaged daughter with him to the show. He wanted to be certain that he kept his commitment despite his personal problems, yet it was obvious that he was a little preoccupied with concern for Jeannie, the woman to whom he's been married since 1964.

Bobby has been singing more than 25 years, his first major hit being "Detroit City," a song that won a Grammy and made the charts for both country and pop. More important, he did it at a time when the market was still quite separated. Most singers went for one or the other and could not get air play on both.

Many of the hits Bobby introduced were obtained from young, relatively unknown musicians whose work he respected. He told me that he felt people such as Willie Nelson, Kris Kristofferson, and Roger Miller were obviously extremely bright, lively individuals when he met them. He had an instinct for both the people and the songs they were creating at a time when few would use their work. Most of the time his instincts were right, the songs becoming major hits. For example, long before Kenny Rogers had heard the song "The Gambler," Bobby Bare was recording it for an album. Of course, he also admitted that there were plenty of times he was either wrong or that a song he did

not think would be successful actually dominated the charts.

I understand the appeal of the young, bright, creative people in show business, including the eccentrics. I love to be around such individuals myself because I feel as though I have so much to learn from them.

Bobby's collaborators have often been rather unusual. For example, a close friend for the last ten years has been Shel Silverstein, the cartoonist whose work includes unusual, humorous poetry and books. Together the two men have produced such albums as "Lullabies, Legends And Lies" and "Down And Dirty." However, these have only been a small portion of his more than 40 albums.

I was reminded of a country version of Bing Crosby when I met Bobby. Like Bing, he wore a hat and had that laid-back attitude despite his success as a publisher, singer, and song writer. His wife, Jeannie, in addition to raising their three kids, runs a gift shop. Playing off on the pronunciation of their name, she has toy bears from all over the world.

On the show, Bobby decided to make a shrimp dish, something about which I have mixed feelings. I find raw shrimp with their odd shape and webbing of veins to be ugly, unpleasant creatures to look at. My feeling probably comes from a past experience.

I was in Norway to make the movie "The Song Of Norway," which was a big thrill for me. We got to spend time in Norway, Denmark, and Sweden, since the film was all shot on location. It was produced by Andrew and Virginia Stone who thought enough of my work to give me the leading role of Nina Greig.

We were in a beautiful hotel where the restaurant had an appetizer of shrimp. I assumed that it would be a simple shrimp cocktail. Instead, the waiter brought out this huge plate of shrimp, each with shell, two little eyes, and little antennae. At that moment I decided that I was going to be very sick. Yet others at the table simply took off their shells, tore off their heads, and ate them as if they were the most wonderful delicacy in the world.

That night I went to the hotel room and had nightmares about the shrimp. They were on the loose, all coming to get me.

Yet because I love shrimp, at least in forms I consider palatable, I did learn to eat shrimp as prepared in Norway. They were absolutely delicious, even if they were served with the heads on!

Wild Rice and Shrimp

As Prepared by Bobby Bare

Ingredients:

1 6-Oz. Pkg. Long Grain Wild
  Rice
1 Cup Shredded Longhorn
  Cheese
1 Lb. Raw Shrimp, Shelled
1 Cup Cream of Mushroom
  Soup, Undiluted
2 Tbsp. Minced Onion
2 Tbsp. Butter
2 Tbsp. Lemon Juice
1½ Tsp. Worcestershire Sauce
½ Tsp. Dry Mustard
¼ Tsp. Pepper
Milk, If Needed

Directions:

Cook 6-oz. pkg. long grain wild rice according to pkg. directions. Preheat oven to 375°.

Shell 1 lb. raw shrimp. Put ½ cup shredded longhorn cheese in large bowl, reserve ½ cup cheese. Add cooked rice, shelled shrimp, cream of mushroom soup, minced onion, butter, lemon juice, Worcestershire sauce, dry mustard and pepper. Mix Well. Pour mixture into 2½ qt. baking dish. If mixture is too thick, add milk, stir. Bake 45 minutes.

4-6 servings

Notes

Phyllis Diller

Phyllis Diller is a long time friend whom I greatly admire. She was raising five children, whom she adored, but had been in an unhappy marriage for many years when she decided that she wanted more from life than just to be a "trapped" housewife. It was 1955, years before there was talk of a women's movement, and the career she chose for herself was almost exclusively male. The idea that a woman in her late 30's might leave her traditional housewife role to step on stage and tell jokes was unheard of. Yet she was so good, the two week contract she was given to appear at San Francisco's Purple Onion was extended to an unprecedented 89 weeks.

Shunning "blue" material, which she does to this day, Phyllis has produced several highly successful books, records, and numerous stage and television appearances. She found that audiences delighted in her discussions of her physical appearance, her sex life, her mythical husband, Fang, her mother-in-law, and her next door neighbor. It was a type of humor to which almost everyone could relate and it assured her success.

What made Phyllis' action so much more remarkable was that there were almost no stand-up comediennes when she began. She and Totie Fields were among the pioneers. Women such as Lucille Ball had long dominated the stage, films, and television, but the world of the stand-up comic was dominated by men when Phyllis started.

I relate strongly to Phyllis. Both of us chose to become performers at a time when there was a chance we would

be severely criticized for doing something different from the norm for women. But as she says, you can't worry about what others will think. You have to get to know yourself, decide what's right for you, and then take the steps necessary to secure your happiness and future. Phyllis says, "The same people that poo-poo what you're doing will be the first to try and borrow money after you've done it!"

I am younger than Phyllis, but I had my children during a similar period. In fact, it was not until my last child was born that there was the first hint of what was to become the women's lib movement. As a result, I, too, suffered a lot of guilt for wanting a career in addition to a family. Thus, Phyllis became a role model for women such as myself.

Phyllis, 37 when she stepped onto the stage of the Purple Onion, was also "too old" for such a career, according to the conventional wisdom of the time. But Phyllis stresses that age is only a number. What matters is how we feel.

For example, my father was 47 years old when he married my mother, then went on to have 10 children. I was the youngest, born when he was 67 years old. Later my mother remarried at the age of 75, this time picking a much younger man — he was only 72. In fact, they were arrested for speeding when they drove to a hotel for their honeymoon. My mother justified their actions to the policeman by saying, "Well, heck, officer, we're in a hurry; we haven't got much time!"

Phyllis likes to joke about her appearance. She claims that she purchased a haunted house in Brentwood Park, Los Angeles, "but the ghosts haven't been back since the night I tried on all my wigs." She also delights in telling a joke that Bob Hope, her mentor over the years, once said about her. According to him, her bra size is "32 long."

In reality, Phyllis is an extremely beautiful woman. I asked her when she decided to become beautiful and she joked, "When I got my sight back."

Part of Phyllis' looks come from the cosmetic surgery she will openly discuss; she is one of the few entertainers to feel comfortable doing so. However, her description of the surgery itself probably is exaggerated. She claims that, in her case, the doctors made some cuts in the base of her neck, attached pulleys and big ropes, then pulled it up as far as it would go!

While Phyllis' drive and talent were the primary reasons for her success, she credits Bob Hope as being one of her earliest supporters. He co-starred with her in three films, *Boy! Did I Get a Wrong Number!, Eight On the Lam,* and *The Private Navy of Sergeant O'Farrell.* She also went to Vietnam with him for one of his Christmas shows, during which Hope claimed that the war could have been ended in three days if Phyllis had been allowed to cook for the enemy.

But the banter between Hope and Phyllis is that of two close friends. How close becomes evident when you enter Phyllis' beautiful home where one of the first things you see is a large portrait of Bob Hope.

What many people do not realize is that there is a more serious side to Phyllis. She is a concert pianist who has appeared with symphony orchestras throughout the country and maintains a room devoted to the composer J.S. Bach in her home.

Phyllis Diller is a remarkable lady and an excellent cook, as the following recipe will prove to you.

Fish Fillets Dijon

As Prepared by Phyllis Diller

Ingredients:

4 Fillets Orange Roughy

COURT BOUILLON:

2 Qts. Cold Water
2 Tbsp. Lemon Juice
1 Cup Dry White Wine
1 Handful Celery Tops
½ Cup Chopped Onion
Salt to Taste

DIJON SAUCE

2 Tbsp. Margarine
1 Tbsp. + 1 Tsp. Cornstarch
1¼ Cups Lowfat Milk
3 Tbsp. Dijon Mustard
1 Tbsp. Lemon Juice

GARNISH:

Paprika, Parsley & Lemon Slices

Directions:

Combine cold water, lemon juice, dry white wine, celery tops, chopped onion and salt to taste in large pot. Bring to boil, reduce heat. Add orange roughy to bouillon. Cook at just below boiling about 5 minutes until fish is done.

Melt margarine in saucepan. Remove from heat and stir in cornstarch until blended. Gradually stir in lowfat milk. Gently boil for 2 minutes, stirring constantly. When thickened, remove from heat and stir in Dijon mustard and lemon juice.

Pour sauce into plate, place fillets on sauce. Garnish with paprika, lemon slices and parsley.

4 servings

Notes

Johnny Lee

t is always a pleasure to work with Johnny Lee. Prior to my show, we had last worked together on "The Mike Douglas Show." He was really hot at that time, having the big hit song from the film *Urban Cowboy*, a single called "Looking For Love." He also liked to pretend he was an ignorant country boy instead of the sophisticated man he is. I remember on that show complimenting him on his cologne which he said, with a wink in his eye, was "purr curdin." It was actually a rather expensive one by Pierre Cardin.

Even as a country boy, Johnny Lee was successful. He was born in Texas City, then raised on a dairy farm in Alta Loma, Texas. By high school he had started a band called Johnny Lee & The Roadrunners which won prizes in contests sponsored by Future Farmers Of America. From there he spent four years in the Navy, including a tour of duty on a guided missile cruiser sailing off the Southeast Asian coast. After that, he returned to East Texas to make his career as a musician.

The first major job Johnny Lee obtained was working as a singer and trumpet player for Mickey Gilley. He worked at the Nestadel Club in Pasadena, Texas, a suburb of Houston. Then, in 1971, Mickey Gilley and Sherwood Cryer opened Gilley's Club five miles from Nestadel. Johnny was fronting Gilley's band and began recording songs two years later. All of them were strong regional hits, quite a few making the national charts. Among them were "Sometimes," "Ramblin' Rose," "Red Sails In The Sunset," and "Country Party."

The reputation he was making caused people to send songs to Johnny Lee to play and record. Often these were in the form of demo tapes, sometimes made professionally and sometimes the result of a couple of amateur song writers singing and using a home tape recorder. Most of the ones that were any good ended being tossed into an old shoe box, in theory to be listened to again.

In 1979, with regional success assured and the shoe boxes filling with discards, a television movie came to Texas for filming. This was the Barbara Eden, Susan St. James picture *The Girls In The Office*. As Johnny explained to me, "They were filming in Houston and came down to Gilley's one night saying that they needed a band for the movie. We all got in a station wagon and headed for the location."

Another movie quickly followed, a film called *Urban Cowboy*. Johnny Lee had no idea what an "urban" cowboy was. "Nobody ever called me urban before," he explained. But he was hired to be a part of the music and he needed some songs. By chance he went to that shoebox, discovering one by a couple of school teachers, one of whom is now a Nashville based song writer. It was a tune called "Looking For Love" which Johnny recorded. His single, plus the "Urban Cowboy" sound track, became top hits. The album went triple platinum in sales. The single was in the top five on both the country and the pop charts. Then an LP called "Looking For Love" went gold, immediately followed by singles "One In A Million," "Bet Your Heart On Me," and "Sounds Like Love," all reaching the top five. Johnny Lee had become an international success, both with the band and on his own.

While on my show, Johnny talked about his daughter, Cherish, about whom he is absolutely crazy. She's a real ham who, in the middle of a show, will say to him, "Daddy, I need to be up there." And Daddy will usually bring her up on stage.

Johnny Lee told me that he was going to make mustard bass. Now growing up on a farm, I was familiar with many of the game fish that are so good to eat, but I had never heard of mustard bass. However, Johnny assured me that

he caught them all the time. Then he went on to tell me about a friend with whom he went fishing who caught one of the largest ever seen. However, there was an old car someone had ditched in the water and the bass became entangled in the rotting hulk. Finally the friend went into the water to try and untangle it, but the bass got away. As soon as the friend reached the buried car, the fish saved itself by rolling up the windows!

That was when I realized that Johnny was making fun of me. Mustard bass refers to the sauce. Any white fish can be used with Johnny's mustard preparation.

Mustard Bass

As Prepared by Johnny Lee

Ingredients:

1 Cup Sour Cream
1 Cup Mustard (American)
1 Sleeve Saltines, Crushed
4 Bass Fillets (or other
  White Fish) Cut into Large
  Chunks (Larger than Bite Size)
Wesson Oil

Directions:

Mix equal parts sour cream and mustard in large shallow bowl. Crush saltines with rolling pin. Cut 4 bass fillets into chunks. Dip fish chunks into sour cream/mustard mixture. Roll chunks in saltines until covered. Chill at least 15 minutes. Deep fry in oil until golden brown. Serve hot or cold.

4 servings

Notes

Jeff Cook

J eff Cook is the versatile guitar, keyboard, fiddle, and vocal performer with the extremely successful group, "Alabama." They are so popular and have won so many awards that people think they have been around for generations. After all, they have won the awards of Entertainer of the Year; Vocal Group of the Year; Album of the Year; Top Album Group; Top Album Artists; Top Singles Group; Overall Top Country Artists, LP & Singles; Overall Top Country Group, LP & Singles; and many more. They have been honored by the Academy of Country Music, "Cash Box," "Billboard," the American Music Awards, "People Magazine," "Music City News," the Country Music Association, and even the International Country Group/Entertainers of the Year— United Kingdom. The list seems endless, boasting more awards than many successful entertainers earn in a life-time. Yet the reality is that they have only been popular since 1979.

Jeff told me that he grew up in Ft. Payne, Alabama, and began jamming with his cousins, Randy Owen and Teddy Gentry, back in 1969. Jeff was working for the government at the time, his cousins employed as carpet layers. They were fairly good, but trying to work on a part-time basis was not very effective. Four years later, in March of 1973, they quit their jobs, moved to Myrtle Beach, South Carolina, and began working six nights a week in local clubs. Their first record was in 1977, but it was not until 1979 when, with the guidance of producer Harold Shedd, they had their first successful single, "I Wanna Come Over,"

followed by "My Home's In Alabama" which made the Top 20.

The Alabama performance is extremely dynamic. They have made a cross-over music approach, bringing a rock style to country music. I remember watching them when we were both on a show called "Live And In Person," a show hosted by my manager at the time.

The problem with a live show is that you never know what you are going to encounter. I had to follow Ziegfried and Roy, an act that used live animals who, through nervousness and natural behavior, left a deposit on the stage. Because there could be no time lost between acts, we had to go on without the mess being mopped.

I went on, accompanied by some dancers, and immediately stepped in the wrong place, my foot slipping out from under me. One of the dancers grabbed me by my belt, keeping me from falling. I don't think the audience noticed, and the experience was one that was not that unusual for live television, but I had a few moments of serious work to pull myself together, not to mention a smelly shoe!

One of the things that amazed me about Jeff was that he plays seven instruments by ear. He never learned to read music, which is something I have encountered occasionally with extremely talented musicians like Jeff in the past. In fact, when I starred in "Fanny," my co-star was the great Ezio Pinza, a man who dominated the field of opera and musical theater for many years. He even sang in several different languages, yet he, too, could not read music. He learned everything by ear, as does Jeff. It's a remarkable ability.

While Jeff has not yet had the acclaim of an Ezio Pinza, the group seems destined for even greater long term success.

FOOD FACTS

Peas have almost as much protein value as an equivalent amount of meat.

•

The biggest producer of bagels in the world is Mattoon, Illinois, where approximately one million bagels a day are baked, frozen and shipped throughout the country.

•

Did you know? Eight pounds of peanut butter is consumed per American per year!

•

When barbarians overthrew Rome in the 5th Century A.D., they demanded land, money, military titles and 3,000 pounds of pepper.

Japanese Shrimp & Vegetables

As Prepared by Jeff Cook

Ingredients:

3 Zucchini Squash
1 Lg. White Onion
1 Pint Mushrooms, Fresh
Soy Sauce
1 Lemon, Halved
½ Stick Butter
Wesson Oil
MSG Seasoning
Salt to Taste
Pepper to Taste
3 Tbsp. Sesame Seeds
½ Lb. Shrimp, Cleaned
Lg. Skillet
Wok

Directions:

Cut zucchini into long strips, then large cubes. Cut onion into large pieces, slice mushrooms. Heat a small amount of oil in wok, add zucchini, mushrooms, onion. Add ¼ stick butter, saute. Pour soy sauce over vegetables to taste. Add seasonings to taste (MSG, salt, and pepper), saute until brown. Sprinkle with sesame seeds, set aside.

In hot skillet, add ¼ stick butter, shrimp, and soy sauce, saute. Squeeze ½ lemon over shrimp while sauteeing, add seasonings to taste (MSG, salt, and pepper). Stir until shrimp is done. Serve shrimp with vegetables.

2-4 servings

Notes

Bill Anderson

Bill Anderson is the host and star of The Nashville Network's extremely successful show, "Fandango," the latest success for a man who is a singer, songwriter, actor, guitarist, and so much more. His style is often low key, several of his records having him reciting the lyrics instead of singing them. As a result, he is called "Whispering Bill," a nickname he has had for so many years, newer fans think that "Whispering" is actually his first name.

Bill is successful in so many different areas related to show business, I asked him about it. He said that he kept broadening himself because of his mother's advice not to put all of his eggs into one basket. This is something that has been a factor for me as well.

When I first started in my career, I was lucky enough to be on Broadway. I loved the stage, but when I became aware of the potential of television, I found that I delighted in that medium as well.

Before I began television in earnest, I had done a few programs such as the old "Steve Allen Show," which was the early version of "The Tonight Show," which now stars Johnny Carson. I also appeared on "The Kate Smith Show" and similar variety programs. Then, when I began appearing first on Jack Paar's show and later, in 1960, when I became the "Today Show" girl, I was hooked. I loved the feel of television, the speed and spontaneity it allowed. Our programs were all live back then, triumphs and disasters equally likely with no way to hide that fact from the audience. Today we can tape a program, correcting any

problem. For example, one one of my shows, a top songwriter/singer momentarily forgot the lyrics to one of his own compositions after he started to play. If you saw the program, you would never know that anything had happened. But back when I began my career, everyone would have shared his embarrassment as he stopped, then started over.

I've always conducted my career with the diversification Bill Anderson discussed. I start with one field, try to become successful in it, then seek the challenge of a new one. I went from stage to television, then gradually added live performances, recordings, commercial, and all the other avenues this business allows. It has also been a way to have longevity which is an important goal for me.

Looking at a video of myself next to Bill brings up a rather unusual circumstance. I have short legs but a very long torso. Men like Bill have bodies that are the reverse, their legs seem to stretch for miles but their torsos are relatively short. As a result, I sometimes appear taller than they do when sitting, yet when we stand, they tower over me.

The television image is so distorted that when people meet me in person, I will get comments such as, "You look so much better in person than you do on television," a statement to which I'm never certain how to react. However, the strangest reaction I ever experienced occurred when I was in a store in Texas. The sales clerk came over to me and discussed what a great fan of mine she was. She had seen or owned everything I had ever done. She was thrilled to have me there as a customer. And then, when I took out my checkbook to pay for my purchase, she suddenly stopped and, in a rather formal voice, said, "Oh, a check? I'm terribly sorry. But do you have any identification?" Oh well, it keeps you humble!

When Bill was on my show, he wore a ring that came from being involved with the 50th anniversary of the Grand Ole Opry in Nashville. To the country music world, being able to sing in the Grand Ole Opry is the same as a classical singer being asked to sing at the Metropolitan Opera.

It had long been one of my dreams to have the honor of singing in the Opry. Eventually that dream came true for me, being able to sing two numbers with my family in the audience. The acoustics were perfect, the stage beautiful, and the audience was one of the most responsive I have ever enjoyed.

Bill made jambalaya on the show and mentioned using the drippings to pour over other foods. That is typical of country cooking. You never waste anything.

I remember when, growing up, my mother would save the hot bacon drippings to pour over the lettuce. It was the forerunner of the hot spinach salad. We also poured it on bread, adding salt and pepper to taste.

Whispering Jambalaya

As Prepared by Bill Anderson

Ingredients:

1½ Lb. Linked Smoked Sausage
  (Pork Preferred),
  Cut in Pieces
1 Pick of the Chicken
  with Bones, Skinned
4 Large Onions, Chopped
1 Large Green Pepper, Chopped
3 Cups Long White
  Cooking Rice, Uncooked
5 Cups Water
Salt to Taste
Pepper to Taste
Garlic Powder to Taste

Directions:

Brown sausage pieces in dutch oven or deep pot. Remove sausage, set aside, don't drain pot. Salt and pepper chicken and brown in same pot. Remove chicken, set aside, don't drain pot. Saute onions and pcppcr in same pot, sprinkling with garlic powder.

Replace all meat in pot, add rice and water, and salt to taste. Bring to full boil, turn to low heat and cover. Cook on low heat for 30 minutes, (don't peek). Serve with tossed salad and rolls or bread.

4-6 servings

Notes

John Sebastian

John Sebastian is an unusual talent. He is a singer, song-writer, arranger, accompanist, film scorer, and so much more. He is also an extremely gentle man who somehow reminded me of a very loving, accepting, caring priest. He is the kind of person with whom you can feel comfortable sharing inner-most feelings, knowing that no matter what you may say, he will not find fault with you. He also was well prepared for the show, having a good recipe and obviously having experience in making it.

John is probably best known as a performer for his part in The Lovin' Spoonful, a very successful rock group of the 1960's. The songs that group produced were frequently million sellers. Among these were ones John wrote, arranged, sang and played, including "Do You Believe In Magic," "Daydream," "Did You Ever Have To Make Up Your Mind," "Nashville Cats," "Younger Girl," "Darlin' Be Home Soon," and "You Didn't Have To Be So Nice."

The work John has done for films covers such a wide range, you may not be able to tell that the same person created the scores. Children know him for having written the music for *The Care Bears Movie* (co-written with Carole King). Adults may remember his first films, beginning in 1964, when he wrote and sang songs for Francis Ford Coppola's *You're A Big Boy Now* and Woody Allen's *What's Up Tiger Lily*. When he wrote the theme song for the television series, "Welcome Back Kotter," the single of that theme became a #1 best seller when it was released.

Rock music was utilized when John wrote the score for

the Broadway show "Jimmy Shine" which starred Dustin Hoffman. He also has written the music for "Strawberry Shortcake's Housewarming Surprise" and some of the songs for "Sesame Street," among numerous others. His personal albums, made in the 1970's, including "She's A Lady," "Younger Generation," and "I Had A Dream" among the hits. And his solo concerts have been so varied that he has been equally at home in Woodstock, Lincoln Center,

Europe, and Japan. In fact, his range is possibly the most varied among the guests I have had on my show.

John's heritage is Irish and Italian, an unusual combination. Mine is more common, a mix of Irish and English. My mother's maiden name was Elder, an English name. My father's grandparents came over from Ireland, one being LaHa and another being HaLa. The family is large enough that periodically after one of my shows, someone in the family would come up and introduce him or herself to me.

My father used to have a wonderful Irish wit as we were growing up and he also had the habit of talking to himself a lot. This was not some mental problem but just his way. However, when someone would tease him, he had a ready comeback. All someone had to do was shout, "Hey, Joe, who are you talking to?" and he would reply, "I'm talking to a damned smart man!"

John and I talked about pasta and the best way to eat it. I like it extremely firm, "el dente" or "to the tooth." However, while firm does not mean hard, I had a rather humorous experience in New York when ordering pasta in an Italian restaurant. I explained to the waiter that I did not want it soft and mushy. I wanted it prepared *el dente.*

The waiter took on a haughty air and said, "Perhaps you would like it *'crudo' — in the box."*

Spaghetti alla Carbonara

As Prepared by John Sebastian

Ingredients:

1 Lb. Pasta
1 Lb. Bacon
6 Eggs
1 Clove Fresh Garlic, Minced
Salt to Taste
Black Pepper, Fresh Ground
2 Cups Parmesan Cheese

Directions:

Prepare pasta according to directions.

While pasta is cooking, beat eggs. Fry bacon, add fresh minced garlic on top of bacon while cooking. Towel dry bacon and cut into small pieces. Dump pasta into large colander and back into pan. Add eggs, bacon, parmesan cheese, then salt & pepper to taste. Cook over medium heat, stirring until eggs have adhered to pasta.

4 servings

Notes

Johnny Rodriguez

Johnny Rodriguez has known the extreme highs and lows of both life and show business. Like myself, he was one of 10 children. But unlike me, he was raised in the small town of Sabinal, Texas, in a four room house just 90 miles from the Mexican border. He was a tough street fighter who ran the streets with a Chicano gang, going to jail four times before he was 18. Yet oddly, Johnny had respect for school, got along well with the Anglos, and was an A-B student, captain of his junior high school football team, a high school letterman, and a church altar boy.

Both Johnny and I always wanted to be in show business despite neither of us coming from families where show business was familiar. Around the age of 11, he discovered that a friend had a guitar and was willing to show him how to use it. He had to walk five miles each way to get to the friend's house and back, but he was determined to learn.

Johnny even managed to put together his own band after learning the guitar. The group was not a particularly good one and had the unlikely name, "The Spocks." They wore pointed ears and dressed somewhat like the character "Mr. Spock" from the "Star Trek" television series. Their music was rock and roll, mostly Beatles and Rolling Stones songs.

The draw of music is universal, both for performers and the audience. It is something we experience in all languages. My reaction to music is very instinctive and I believe music is a great healer. It can set off emotions or heal hurt emotions; music is a gift from God.

In fact, it was Johnny's singing in jail after being arrested

for stealing and barbecuing a goat that led to his being discovered as an entertainer. A Texas Ranger named Juaquin Jackson heard Johnny sing in the jail cell and was extremely impressed. He introduced Johnny to Happy

Shahan, a man who owned a western tourist ranch and knew many people in the music business.

Johnny obtained a job with Shahan, working summers in 1970 and 1971. "I wrangled horses, drove a stagecoach, cleaned out restrooms, sang, anything. I did those gunfight shows in the street where we would shoot each other." He also met Tom T. Hall and Bobby Bare.

Tom T. Hall was so impressed with Johnny that he told him that he would like to hire him for the band at some time in the future. Johnny assumed he was just being nice, returning home and going to work in the construction business with his father and brother. However, when both his father and brother died, Johnny, then 20 years old, decided to go to Nashville.

Johnny tried to get in touch with both Bobby Bare and Tom T. Hall after his arrival. He was staying in the Sam Davis Hotel and had just $14, four shirts, and three pairs of pants to his name. He didn't think he stood much of a chance at getting a job in the music business, but he felt that Nashville was where he would eventually succeed. To his surprise, Tom T. Hall left a message for him to meet him at Linebaugh's Restaurant on lower Broadway.

By coincidence, Tom T. had just lost a guitar player and called Happy Shahan to try to learn where Johnny was living so he could offer him a job. Johnny moved into Tom T.'s home until he could make some money and learn the music, then went on the road.

For the next year Johnny was a singer and semi-secretary for Tom T. Hall. On the road, Tom T. would have Johnny write down lines and ideas while he composed new songs. Johnny got to see an additional creative side to the business, a side that also fascinated him. This would eventually result in his writing his own music.

At the end of that year, Johnny was asked to sing for Roy Dea, a staff producer for Mercury Records. The result was a recording contract and his first success, "Pass Me By." Then came "You Always Come Back to Hurting Me," the first of 11 straight #1 singles on the charts, some of which he wrote or co-wrote. Then he had an album entitled "Introducing Johnny Rodriguez" which became #1 on all three major charts. And by 1973, Johnny was nominated as Male Vocalist Of The Year by the Country Music Association.

It would seem that the honors and success came too easily and too fast for Johnny. In a relatively short period of time his marriage fell apart, he left country music to sing rock and roll, he became a cocaine user, and he injured himself in a karate class when he tried to do a standing back flip.

There was a period when Johnny began to lose all his money and his voice. He was an emotional and physical wreck. Eventually he headed for a farm in the remote country of Ashland City, Tennessee. He began to come to some self-understanding and return to better values. "It's all in your head, all in your attitude about yourself," he explained. "If you think you can't do it, you can't. If you think you can, you can."

The emotional and physical recovery turned Johnny back to country music, his first love. He had shown skill in his rock music recordings, but there was none of the genius that marked his other work. He realized where he belonged. He happily explains, "I've got a second chance. I made it through. I feel that way because I've got my health back. I'm back in touch. I'm on the street again."

Now Johnny is rapidly returning to the top of the country charts.

Carne Guisada
As Prepared by Johnny Rodriguez

Ingredients:

Steak for Four
  (any tender cut, even round)
2 Lg. Onions, Cut into Chunks
¼ Cup Flour
1 Can Whole Tomatoes, 19 Oz.
1 Doz. Corn Tortillas, Steamed
1 Pkg. Long Grain White Rice,
  8 Oz., Uncooked
1 Clove Garlic, Minced
2 or 3 Whole Tomatoes
  from Can
¼ Cup Red & Green
  Bell Peppers, Chopped Fine
Liquid for Rice:
  ½ Water & ½ Tomato Juice
  from Canned Tomatoes
¼ Cup Wesson Oil
Salt, Pepper, and Cumin

Directions:

Cut steak into cubes, and brown in frying pan with ¼ cup oil over med./low heat. Add onions, cook until tender. Sprinkle flour over steak and onions, and stir in thoroughly. Cut 1 lg. can whole tomatoes into chunks and add to mixture, add enough juice from can to make a smooth sauce (about ¼ cup). Add salt and pepper to taste, and 1 tsp. cumin.

Fry 1 pkg. long grain white rice until browned with hot oil and minced clove of garlic. Add red and green bell peppers, chopped fine, and 2 or 3 whole canned tomatoes, squashed. Add enough liquid for rice; ½ water and ½ tomato juice from can. Cook over medium heat uncovered until liquid is absorbed. Serve steak dish with rice, tortillas, hot sauce and pinto beans.

4 servings

Notes

Rosey Grier

osey Grier is a remarkable giant of a man. Many people recognize the 6'5" Grier from his days as a professional football player with the New York Giants and the Los Angeles Rams. They also remember him as a supporter of the late Robert Kennedy when Kennedy ran for President. It was Grier who disarmed assassin Sirhan Sirhan after Sirhan shot Kennedy during an appearance in Los Angeles.

But the remarkable aspect of Rosey Grier is his versatility and caring. He is an actor who has appeared on numerous television programs as well as such films as *Roots*, *Skyjacked*, and *In Cold Blood*, among others. He authored the book "Needlepoint For Men," and eventually he bacame an ordained minister. The latter occurred when he became frustrated with the ways in which programs for the impoverished were being run. He felt that all they did was keep people alive. They did not enable them to leave their grinding poverty. As a result, he created "Are You Committed" which is based in Los Angeles.

The "Are You Committed" training center in downtown Los Angeles was opened on February 25, 1984. There are free educational and spiritual training classes for the young. Computer literacy training is provided since a knowledge of computers is critical for future jobs in the United States. There is a job bank to both teach job skills and work with business leaders to provide skilled employees. There is also a clothing store, the AYC Outlet, that provides low cost clothing and training in retail sales. There is remedial reading training and spiritual guidance. It is a remarkable

program and a remarkable crusade, for a man who has known so many successes in so many different fields. His heart is obviously just as big as his body.

I was deeply touched by the story of his relationship with his wife, Margie, who is both his first and his second wife. There was a period when he was famous, successful, and certain that he had been missing something special in life. He had not yet found the spiritual values that guide him now and he was out for whatever pleasures he could get. He divorced Margie and began playing the field, certain that there was something special waiting for him in life. What he discovered was that the greatest joy he had known with another person came only when he had been with Margie. He returned to her, admitted the mistake he had made, sought her forgiveness, and remarried her. They have been extremely close ever since.

While Rosey's story about his relationship with his wife was deeply moving for me, on the lighter side, the idea of unrealistic expectations reminds me of a situation that occurred when I was on the original "Hollywood Squares" with Paul Lynde. Paul was an extremely funny comedian with a quick mind who made a very funny, yet somewhat poignant comment concerning relationships in answer to a question. The question that was raised was, "What are two things you should never do on your honeymoon night?"

Paul answered, "You musn't point and laugh!"

Rosey's commitment to the inner city kids has impressed me greatly. The one message he tries to get across, and it is a concept that I have had to learn as well, is that you are responsible for your own life. It is too easy to blame someone or something else for your circumstances. But I have learned that you can't change anyone else, regardless of the great amounts of time and energy you spend trying to do so; you can only change yourself!

Part of Rosey's motivation came because he had to begin working in the fields at the age of 5. He was hot, miserable, and knew that there had to be a better way. Having started working on the farm when I was 8, helping with the crops, I know exactly what he means. Sometimes sweat and exhaustion can be great motivators.

FOOD FACTS

Did you know — squash is a Massachusetts Indian word meaning raw or uncooked.

•

What spice grows on trees and is called Pimento in its native Jamaica? Allspice.

•

The average American eats approximately 50 lbs. of red meat and 50 lbs. of chicken per year, but only 13 lbs. of fish.

•

George Washington Carver, a botanist, discovered more than 300 uses for peanuts, including such non-food uses as shoe polish and shampoo.

File Gumbo

As Prepared by Rosey Grier

Ingredients:

STOCK:

6 Cups Water
6 Chicken Bouillon Cubes
4 Tsp. Worcestershire Sauce
1 Clove

GUMBO:

6 Green Onions
2 Cups Chopped Okra
1 Tbsp. Bacon Fat
1 Cup Chopped Tomatoes
1 Pod Red Pepper
1 Pre-Cooked Chicken,
Skinned and Chopped
Bite-Size
1 Green Pepper, Chopped
½ Tsp. Thyme
1 Bay Leaf
1 Tsp. Salt
½ Lb. Shrimp
½ Lb. Cooked Crab
2 Hot Links or Hot Italian
Sausages (Cooked)
1 Tbsp. File

Directions:

Mix water, bouillon cubes, Worcestershire sauce and clove to make stock.

Clean and chop onions, reserving green tops. Saute with okra in bacon fat. Add tomatoes and green pepper, cook 5 minutes, add to stock. Add green onion tops (cut into strips), file, thyme, bay leaf, red pepper pod, and salt to stock. Heat to boiling and simmer 45 minutes. Add shrimp, chicken, crab and hot links. Simmer about 1 hour. Serve with rice.

6 servings

Notes

Faron Young

aron Young is a remarkable entertainer who has been delighting audiences for over 30 years. He has had more than 80 records on the top five of the country music charts and is well known for such songs as "Hello, Walls," "I Miss You Already," "Sweethearts Or Strangers," "Wine Me Up," "Going Steady," and numerous others. He has hosted "Nashville Now" on The Nashville Network, worked with Willie Nelson at Willie's annual 4th of July picnic, won the Tex Ritter Award for his contributions to country music, and earned numerous other honors and successes.

It is interesting to note that Faron came late to country music beginning his singing career after high school. He sang from the time he was young, though, and one of his teachers, the high school football coach, delighted in hearing him sing.

Faron loved football but was too small to be taken very seriously. He was determined to play in high school, though, so he used his singing voice for blackmail. He told the coach that if he did not get to play football, he would refuse to sing. Faron quickly made the team.

That story reminded me of my high school experience with one of my most favorite teachers in the whole world, Father O'Bryan. He was a former Navy chaplain, a tough veteran whom I adored.

I was pretty mischievous in high school, always talking and laughing, and that would frequently get me into trouble. Father O'Bryan used to say, "Florence, take a walk!" That meant that I was thrown out of class, and the only way I could get back in was to sing a song. He loved Irish songs and I was only too willing to oblige.

Father O'Bryan did more than just let me sing to return to class. I remember one time when I cheated on my geometry exam. I was not very good at geometry and I was even worse at cheating. Had I copied only a few of the answers, I would have had some questions right and others wrong. My cheating would not have been obvious. Instead, I copied all the correct answers, turning in a paper that was perfect, an impossibility for me!

Father O'Bryan called me out of the lunch line after grading the papers and said, "You cheated on that geometry exam, didn't you?"

"Yes, Father, I did," I told him.

Maybe he felt sorry for me and maybe he was pleased that I told the truth. Whatever the case, he did pass me in the course, one of many kindnesses for which I will always be grateful.

Faron Young's school experiences may have differed from mine, but we both share what I consider an important attitude in show business. We both recognize how important the fans are to our success.

Too often when people are starting out, they are extremely nice to their fans. Then, when they make it, they decide that they don't have time any more. They can't take time to sign autographs. They won't respond to letters.

Faron and I both have the attitude that the fans are important. If someone takes the time to write you a letter and they put a return address on it, then they deserve an answer.

The stew Faron made was typical of the facet of country cooking, the ability to keep adding to the pot to serve your friends—an important yet often inexpensive and easy way to be hospitable to unexpected and hungry guests.

The importance of food to country people often comes from their poverty. I can remember when I was going to high school, I lived in Kentucky but rode the bus to the nearest school which was in Rockport, Indiana. There was a place called "The Modern," a cafe at the stop where you had to change buses.

I remember one day when I had enough money to buy myself a piece of pie, a treat that was heaven for me. Yet when I got down to the end, the last few bites, I noticed a creature in the pie. It was some sort of large insect, perhaps the least appetizing choice of filling imaginable.

I seriously considered screaming and, today, I know that such a sight would instantly take away my appetite. However, I decided to remain calm, calling over the waitress and showing her my discovery. She apologized, told me I would not be charged, took away the pie, and brought me a second piece. Being hungry all the time, I did not think about the general cleanliness of the baker. Instead I delighted in that second piece, relishing every bite and, fortunately, not discovering the creature's mate.

Hillbilly Stew

As Prepared by Faron Young

Ingredients:

3 Lbs. Sirloin Tips
2 Tbsp. Wesson Oil
2 Cans Whole Tomatoes
1 Can Okra
3 Cans Whole Potatoes
1 Can Succotash
2 Lg. Onions, Sliced
3 Tbsp. Garlic Powder
1 Tbsp. Garlic Salt
2 Tbsp. Sugar
3 Tsp. Black Pepper
1/3 Cup Worcestershire Sauce

Directions:

Brown sirloin tips in oil 5 minutes. Cut potatoes into chunks. In a large pot, combine steak, tomatoes, okra, potatoes, succotash, onions, garlic powder, garlic salt, sugar, pepper, and Worcestershire sauce. Bring to boil, reduce heat, simmer 30 - 45 minutes.

6 servings

Notes

Jimmie Walker

Jimmie Walker was one of my most difficult guests, a wild, spontaneous actor with whom I last worked on "Hollywood Squares." He was the first guest to deviate from the recipe, playing for laughs.

Jimmie Walker has had a lot of laughs over the years, but the reality of his childhood is such that he is obviously a remarkable man. He was born in the South Bronx, an area where many of the buildings are burned out and poverty was pervasive. School was unimportant to the boys growing up there, basketball being the one game that could get you a high paying career. However, while Jimmie thought he was training himself for a position with the New York Knicks, the reality was that he was neither particularly tall nor a very good player. Even worse, at 15 years of age, he could neither read nor write. He decided to leave school, getting jobs first in the mail room at Johns-Manville and, later, as a delivery boy at the Grand Union Market. His highest salary was $47, before taxes. He had no future.

It was two years later when Jimmie accepted the reality that if you could not read or write, you could do next to nothing in life. He saw other men coming in, buying steaks, produce and wine for a dinner, spending as much as $14 for a meal. He decided he wanted to be able to earn money the way they did. He asked his boss if he could leave work slightly early each shift, then went to Theodore Roosevelt High School, to earn his diploma at night. From there he joined the federally funded program, Search for Education, Evaluation and Knowledge (SEEK). He was given $50 a week for living expenses, textbooks, and the chance to increase his education.

Jimmie became a radio announcer and learned engineering at the RCA Technical Institute. It took him two tries, but he eventually earned his First Class engineering license, gaining a job at WRBR radio as a part-time engineer making $100 per week. He also continued with SEEK, studying mathematics and literature. He even discovered previously unknown writing skills, including the ability to create comedy. By 1967, he was earning $250 per week at WMCA radio and on his way to becoming a star.

Jimmie's style is often aggressive and outrageous. He talked non-stop, almost shouting at the camera. He reminded me of an incident when I was a frequent guest on the Dean Martin Show. We were singing a duet during rehearsal and I guess I got a little carried away. Apparently, I was belting out a song a little louder than Dean wanted because he turned to me and said, "You don't have to shout, Florence. You've already got the job." Working with Jimmie, I sometimes felt I should tell him that he also already had the job.

Jimmie's first break came on "The Jack Paar Show," a forerunner of the current Johnny Carson Show. Jimmie's friends, including such new stars as Bette Midler, David Brenner, and Steve Landesberg, had appeared on the show and requested that he be given a chance. After that appearance, he was suddenly appearing regularly on television and in night clubs. Then Norman Lear offered him a lead in the comedy series, "Good Times," and he was on his way to the top. The catch phrase used in the show, "Dyn-o-mite!" became a part of the popular culture of the period. There were even Jimmie Walker dolls that spoke the word. In fact, he was so successful that Time Magazine named him Comedian of the Decade.

By the time Jimmie was on my show, he had established himself in films, television, and night clubs. He had worked in 49 of the 50 states, made a successful record, and appeared in several commercials. He also has an excellent mind for business, making him wealthy enough that he could reture if he so chose. In all, for a man who could not read or write at 15, his is a remarkable success story.

FOOD FACTS

The only commercial producer of mangoes in the continental United States is — Southern Florida.

•

In 1692, a London grocer sold a rare, expensive new fruit which pharmacists complained was a dangerous drug — the banana!

•

According to the 1985 Guinness Book of World Records, the world's best-selling cookie is the Oreo!

•

The inventor of peanut butter was a St. Louis physician who ground peanuts for elderly patients who needed an easily digestable source of protein.

Barbecued Spareribs

As Prepared by Jimmie Walker

Ingredients:

3 Lbs. Spareribs
¼ Cup Cider Vinegar
2 Tbsp. Sugar
¼ Tsp. Cayenne
1 Chopped Onion
½ Cup Water
1 Tbsp. Dry Mustard
½ Cup Crushed Pineapple
¾ Cup Catsup
2 Tbsp. Worcestershire Sauce
½ Tsp. Pepper
1 Tsp. Salt

Directions:

Preheat oven to 325°. Combine in saucepan: cider vinegar, sugar, cayenne, chopped onion, water, dry mustard, and crushed pineapple. Simmer 20 minutes, uncovered.

Add catsup and Worcestershire sauce, bring to boil, remove from heat. Salt and pepper spareribs. Place in a pan with small amount of water and bake covered at 325° F for 1 hour.

Drain ribs, cook over charcoal, basting frequently with sauce. Serve with stuffed eggs and slaw.

4-6 servings

Notes

Index

Anderson, Bill 201-204
Apples, Fall-Baked, Sausage Filled, 151
Axton, Hoyt 177-180
Barbecued Chicken 35
Barbecued Spareribs 223
Bare, Bobby 185-188
Beef,
   and Biscuit Casserole 87
   Cheeseburger Noodles 51
   Chili Beef Stir-Fry 155
   Curry Pepper Steak 15
   Hamburger a la Brandy 179
   Hillbilly Stew 219
   Steak 95
   Stuffed Bell Peppers 31
   Texas Tacos 57
   Bombay Beef 129
Beef and Biscuit Casserole 87
Beef Bombay 129
Bellamy Brothers, The 21-24
Blackstone, Harry, Jr. 93-96
Bonsall, Joe 105-108
Broccoli Chicken Thighs 111
Brown, Jim Ed 145-148
Brown, T. Graham 113-116
Carne Guisada 211
Casseroles,
   Beef and Biscuit 87
   Creole Egg 83
   Wild Duck Casserole 147
Cheeseburger Noodles 51
Cheesy "Spam" Bake 115
Chicken,
   and Shrimp Supreme 163
   Barbecued 35
   Broccoli Chicken Thighs 111
   Chinese Chicken Salad 69

Enchiladas 103
File Gumbo 215
Italian 143
Jambalaya, Whispering 203
Mississippi Fried 137
Nitty Gritty Dirt Chicken 183
Chicken and Shrimp Supreme 163
Chicken Enchiladas 103
Chili Beef Stir-Fry 155
Chinese Chicken Salad 69
Clower, Jerry 135-138
Cole Slaw 35
Cook, Jeff 197-200
Country Breakfast 27
Country Gravy 11
Country Summer Day Dinner 91
Creole Egg Casserole 83
Curry Pepper Steak 15
Dean, Jimmy 149-152
Diller, Phyllis 189-192
Dorito Chip Salad 47
Duck,
   Wild Duck Casserole 147
Eden, Barbara 131-134
Eggs,
   Creole Casserole 83
   Country Breakfast 27
Emery, Ralph 49-52
Enchiladas Verdes 125
Fall-Baked Apples 151
Fender, Freddie 117-120
Fettucini Alfredo 39
File Gumbo 215
Fish,
   Chicken and Shrimp Supreme 163
   File Gumbo 215
   Fillets Dijon 191
   Florentine 43

Mustard Bass 195
Salmon with Lemon Basil Sauce 159
Stir-Fry Shrimp 23
Wild Rice and Shrimp 187
Fish Fillets Dijon 191
Fish Florentine 43
Frizzell, David 123-126
Game Hens, Stuffed Cornish 61
Gatlin, Larry 63-66
Gay, Don 55-58
Grier, Rosey 213-216
Hamburger,
   Cheeseburger Noodles 51
   Hamburger a la Brandy 179
Hamburger a la Brandy 179
Hillbilly Stew 219
Homestyle Potato Soup 171
Italian Chicken 143
Italian Dishes,
   Eggplant Casserole 107
   Fettucini Alfredo 39
   Italian Chicken 143
   Lasagna 79
   Spaghetti 175
   Spaghetti alla Carbonara 207
Italian Eggplant Casserole 107
Jambalaya, Whispering 203
Japanese Shrimp and Vegetables 199
Johnson, Michael 153-156
Lamb Ka-Bob 133
Lee, Johnny 193-196
Lasagna 79
Lindsey, George 33-36
Mandrell, Irlene 17-20
McEuen, John 181-184
Mexican,
   Carne Guisada 211

Chicken Enchiladas 103
Enchiladas Verdes 125
Migas Rancheras 119
Texas Hot Tamale Pie 75
Texas Tacos 57
Tortilla Soup 65
Migas Rancheras 119
Mississippi Fried Chicken 137
Mustard Bass 195
Nabors, Jim 67-71
Nelson, Willie 9-12
Nitty Gritty Dirt Chicken 183
Pasta,
    Cheeseburger Noodles 51
    Fettucini Alfredo 39
    Lasagna 79
    Spaghetti 175
    Spaghetti alla Carbonara 207
Pork,
    Country Summer Day Dinner 91
    Pork 'n' Kraut 167
Pearl, Minnie 81-84
Pork 'n' Kraut 167
Potato Chips 179
Potato Salad 91
Potato Soup 171
Rabbitt, Eddie 127-130
Redenbacher, Orville 141-144
Reed, Robert 85-88
Reese, Della 109-112
Rice,
    Wild Rice and Shrimp 187
Riley, Jeannie C. 73-76
Rodriguez, Johnny 209-212
Salad,
    Chinese Chicken 69
    Dorito Chip 47

Potato 91
Salmon with Lemon Basil Sauce 159
Sauces,
    Alfredo 39
    Country Gravy 11
    Dijon, 191
    Florentine 43
    Lemon Basil 159
Sausage,
    Fall-Baked Apples, Sausage Filled 151
    File Gumbo 215
    Jambalaya, Whispering 203
Seals, Dan 169-172
Sebastian, John 205-208
Sheppard, T.G. 161-164
Shrimp,
    Chicken and Shrimp Supreme 163
    Japanese Shrimp and Vegetables 199
    Stir-Fry Shrimp 23
    Wild Rice and, 187
Skaggs, Ricky 25-28
Soup,
    File Gumbo 215
    Potato 171
    Tortilla 65
Spaghetti 175
Spaghetti alla Carbonara 207
Spam,
    Cheesy "Spam" Bake 115
Spareribs, Barbecued 223
Steak 95
Steak Stew 19
Sterban, Richard 77-80
Stew,
    Hillbilly 219
    Jambalaya 203
    Steak 19

Stir-Fry Shrimp 23
Stuffed Bell Peppers 31
Stuffed Cornish Game Hens 61
Sylvia 173-176
Texas Hot Tamale Pie 75
Texas Tacos 57
Tillis, Mel 89-92
Thomas, B.J. 37-40
Tillotson, Johnny 157-160
Tortilla Soup 65
Tucker, Tanya 45-48
Varney, Jim 13-16
Veal,
    Wiener Schnitzel 99
Vegetable Dishes,
    Italian Eggplant Casserole 107
    Stuffed Bell Peppers 31
Walker, Jimmie 221-224
Waltrip, Darrell 41-44
West, Dottie 29-32
West, Shelly 97-100
Whispering Jambalaya 203
White, Sharon 165-168
Whites, The 101-104
Wiener Schnitzel 99
Wild Duck Casserole 147
Wild Rice and Shrimp 187
Williams, Barry 59-62
Young, Faron 217-220